ReConnecting

A Wesleyan Guide
For the Renewal of Our
Congregation

ReConnecting

A Wesleyan Guide
For the Renewal
of Our Congregation

Rob Weber

Abingdon Press

ReConnecting: A Wesleyan Guide for the Renewal of Our Congregation

Participant's Guide and Daily Journal: ISBN 0-687-06535-6
Leader's Guide with DVD: ISBN 0-687-02234-2

Scripture quotations designated (NRSV) are from the New Revised Standard Version of the Bible, copyright © 1989, by the Division of Christian Education of the National Council of the Churches of Christ in the United States of America. Used by permission.

Scripture quotations designated (NIV) are from the Holy Bible, *New International Version* copyright © 1973, 1978, 1984 by the International Bible Society. Used by permission of Zondervan Bible Publishers.

This book is printed on acid-free, recycled paper.

05 06 07 08 09 10 11—10 9 8 7 6

MANUFACTURED IN THE UNITED STATES OF AMERICA

For my parents, Ted and Mudie Weber,
who connected me with the richness of life, history, and family.

CONTENTS

Getting Started

What's it all about?

Reconnecting responds to the cries and questions about ways in which United Methodist churches can be more effective in this rapidly changing world, while remaining strong and even renewing a connection with our tradition and heritage. *Reconnecting* is a seven-week series designed for use with groups in congregations who desire to be faithful and growing at this important time in history.

Disney's *The Lion King* was a smash hit as a movie and as a play on Broadway. The story centers on Simba, a lion cub who is destined to become the king. Simba is forced to flee his home (the Pridelands) because his evil uncle, Scar, convinced him that he was in some way responsible for his father's death. Simba grows up in a foreign setting and gradually forgets that he was originally created to become king. One day, Simba has an encounter with Rafiki the baboon, a wise medicine-man character, who lures him deep into the forest by telling Simba that he knows where his father is. Simba, believing that his father is dead, follows the baboon and finally comes to a small pool of water surrounded by high grass. Rafiki tells him to look in the pool. Simba is disappointed when all he sees is his own reflection—but Rafiki tells Simba to "*Look harder…*" With a touch of the baboon's staff, the water stirs, and when the reflection comes back into focus, it is not his own reflection that he sees, but the reflection of his father. "*You see,*" says the wise baboon, "*He lives in you.*" The image in the water then speaks to Simba and tells him "*You have forgotten me and you have forgotten who you are.*" He reminds his son that he is destined to be so much more than what he has become. After his encounter with his father's reflection, Simba is changed, and he heads straight back to the Pridelands to defeat Scar and take his place as king. Simba re-connected with his identity and purpose, and it changed the direction and outcome of his life.

As Jesus begins his ministry, he too has an encounter with a pool of water. Immediately following his baptism, Jesus hears the words "*You are my beloved son, with whom I am well pleased.*" This encounter is a defining moment for Jesus. It is a moment that imprints on his mind and soul who he is and what his life is for. When we engage in ministry it is important to remember that our ministry emerges from who we are and who it is that we have been created to become. Directly following this defining moment, Jesus sets off into the wilderness for a period of preparation. He spends forty days in prayer, meditation and fasting. After his time of preparation, armed with a connection to his identity as God's child, and a clear sense of purpose and mission, he is able to embark on a ministry that changes the world. From time to time it is important that we rekindle that sense of memory and identity that provide us with a reminder of what it is that we have been created for.

ReConnecting is a seven-week journey designed to help individuals and congregations encounter a fresh sense of identity, memory, and place in God's story. It is not a "church program," but rather a journey to be shared. The videos are not a series of lectures, or "talking heads." Instead, video becomes an instrument for creating shared experience. Video storytelling, interviews, and on-location filming at many of the historical locations important to the birth of the Methodist movement allow the participants to travel together to different places and to hear different perspectives from a variety of church leaders and theologians. Through *ReConnecting*, participants will experience a new or renewed connection with their identity, purpose, and place in the ongoing story of God's transforming and redeeming work in the world.

How is it used?

The *ReConnecting* experience is adaptable for a variety of settings.

- It is helpful for use with congregations that have been in existence for many years and need to share an experience of remembering who they are for the purpose of renewal or revitalization. (Think about what the remembering did for Simba.)

- It is helpful for congregations that are preparing to discern or rekindle vision, or are about to embark on a long range planning process.

- It is helpful in training leaders in the congregation by providing a deeper understanding of identity, direction, spiritual disciplines, and the purpose of the church.

- It is helpful for developing small groups and small-group leaders.

- It is a helpful launching pad for a variety of different adult spiritual formation experiences: Bible studies, spiritual formation groups, or covenant disciple groups in the Wesleyan tradition.

- It provides postmodern seekers with an experiential entry point into connection with the personally and socially transforming life of the early Wesleyan movement.

- *ReConnecting* is suitable for use as a congregation-wide emphasis, a small group resource, or an individual devotional guide. Instructions for planning and implementing *ReConnecting* for churches in a variety of settings is available on the DVD, or by download at www.cokesbury.com.

What can we expect?

Several congregations participated as test groups as *ReConnecting* was developed. It was used in large, medium and small congregations. Some churches were new with a low average age, and some tested had almost 200 years of history. In each setting the congregations experienced a burst of excitement and energy that served to launch them forward in ministry.

Results

One of the churches which used *ReConnecting* as a congregation-wide experience during the fall, with approximately 150 adults participating, shared these results:

- Eight new individuals/couples signed up for small-group leader training.
- Six participants formed a task group to develop a new series of adult education opportunities to accompany the new worship service.
- Twenty participants expressed interest in participating in the new educational opportunities.
- A visioning taskforce was established to discern strategies and direction for the church.
- Fifteen participants requested a program to help them understand ministry according to spiritual gifts.
- Eighteen participants registered for Disciple Bible Study.

- Twenty-two participants registered for a spiritual growth group.
- A group was formed to assess what was necessary to facilitate developing ministries that would reach more effectively beyond the walls of the church.
- Interest was expressed in exploring the possibility of developing a second site for the church to enable more people to be reached and the church to grow in ministry, mission, and members.

Other Comments about ReConnecting

"It helped me understand what the Church is all about!" *Marty, age 28*

"Wow! So that's who we are. I'm glad to be part of a church that can help change my life and make a difference in the world." *Shane, age 31*

"I learned more about what it means to be a United Methodist Christian during *ReConnecting* than I have during my whole life as a church member." *Suzie, age 45*

"*ReConnecting* became the "buzz-word" at our church. People became excited about the future of our ministry. It was just what we needed." *Linda, age 46*

"I've gained a new perspective on ministry beyond the walls of the church and I can't wait to get involved." *John, age 47*

"Now I understand why some churches are developing new styles of worship in order to reach new generations of people." *Bob, age 72*

If you or your congregation are longing for something that will help create a climate of excitement, energy, purpose, passion and connection with the changing world and our changeless God, then get ready to begin this journey of reconnection.

LET'S BEGIN

Maybe you have felt this before...The padded bar shuts across your waist with a muffled metallic sound, and with a slight jerk, you begin to roll out of the station. Filled with tentative anticipation, you proceed towards the base of the first hill. The free-gliding train switches masters, from the gravity drawing it downward to the rickety-sounding chain that grabs hold and brings it up to the top of the hill. There, in one pregnant moment, you survey your future—twisted, fast, scary, exciting, and exhilarating. That moment is a moment of release. It is a moment of trust as well as fear. Somewhere in the midst of those feelings is the edge of life for which we are willing to pay dearly, over and over. It is a moment of giving up control, and yet being able to trust that, in the midst of the excitement, you will remain safe. In order to enjoy the ride, you must let go. As we prepare to embark on a journey together, I believe we may experience some of the same feelings. We will be taking a journey together through history and our rapidly changing society. We will be covering a lot of ground in a short period of time. This can be a time of joy and excitement. I anticipate that you won't merely hold on tight and endure, but that you will let go and enjoy the ride.

Through the process of *ReConnecting*, I pray that you will be able to trust the God who holds us even in the midst of the twists and turns of life. So climb in. Take a seat. Buckle up. Put your hands in the air and give yourself to the journey.

How to use this manual

This manual will be companion and guide as you journey through *ReConnecting*. It is designed to help you hear from God through the process of reading, reflecting, and journaling. The next seven weeks can be a great experience for you and your companions. This experience has the potential to help deepen the connection that you have with God and with the life of the Church. The potential effectiveness depends upon you and the willingness you bring to participate. If you approach the readings, the journaling, and the group sessions with openness of heart and mind, and an active willingness to seek God's will for your life and the life of the church, you will not be disappointed.

The readings are from three sources. Each day, you will encounter:

- God's Words through Scripture;

- Wesley's Words through excerpts from his sermons,[1] and

- Contemporary Words, commentary to help provide direction for journaling and meditation.

Give yourself enough time with the readings to let the thoughts of the biblical writers and Wesley begin to stir thoughts in you. What were the they facing in life as they wrote these words? Whom did they have in mind as an audience? How is my situation similar or different from that of the author? These were real people with a passion for God, much like you and me. Ask yourself, "What were they trying to communicate and what does it say to me?"

It is important to understand that the readings are not chosen to communicate information; they are chosen to aid in transformation. Rather than providing commentary on the readings, their interpretation is left to you. The second dimension of the workbook, journaling, will help facilitate that process.

Journaling may be a new experience for you. It may seem strange to have a blank page staring at you with no direction about what to write. There is, however, a reason that the book was developed in this way. Instead of reading the passages in order to respond to a particular set of questions, or to get the "right" answer, you have an opportunity to listen, reflect, and see how God might speak to you personally in your own unique situation.

As you reflect on what you have read, you might want to write a *prayer*. The prayer could be carefully written, or simply an outpouring of your thoughts. You might want to imagine yourself writing a *letter* to the author of the passage, to Wesley, or even to God. Your writing might be in the form of *questions* directed to God, Wesley, yourself, your church, or the people outside the walls of the church. What might God put in a letter to you or to your church? Be creative. Be thoughtful. Be honest. Make the serious effort and watch the way God will begin to communicate with you through your own writings.

Schedule time for your reading and reflection. Don't make the mistake of thinking that you can just fit it in somewhere. Follow the example of John Wesley and get "methodical" about your time with God. Put it on your calendar and stick to it. If you schedule your time as an appointment with God, you will find it more difficult to skip. I believe that there is a God, and that God has real interaction with people. God's activity is not just something that happened way back then but continues here and now...and if we believe that, then, here and now, through this time together, we can CONNECT!

Using the Leader's Guide with DVD

The *Participant's Guide and Daily Journal* provides group participants with daily readings on each session topic, and the daily journaling exercises invite them to connect the biblical and Wesleyan principles with their own spiritual journey and the life of their congregation. This same material is also included in the printed *Leader's Guide*. The *Leader's Guide* also includes a DVD-ROM that contains everything you need during the session—including music, video, and presentation slides—for leading the *ReConnecting* experience. The additional resources found on the DVD are:

- A video introduction to the series;

- Seven professional twenty-minute video segments for viewing in group sessions;

- Seven music tracks for use in group worship and centering;

- Printable leader's guide with directions for planning and implementing the *ReConnecting* experience;

- Additional text files for use in getting the word out through bulletins, newsletters, posters and mailings;

- Files for overhead transparencies or PowerPoint® slides for use in class presentation;

- Suggestions for strategic planning and visioning.

WHAT ARE THE ADDITIONAL RESOURCES ON THE DVD?

The following is a list of the folders included on the DVD and a brief description of the files contained in each:

Leader's Guide

The *Leader's Guide* is included on the DVD as a PDF file (**Leader's Guide.pdf**). To open this file, you will need to have Adobe© Acrobat© Reader installed on your computer. (See page 13 for instructions about installing Acrobat Reader.) The *Leader's Guide* contains step-by-step instructions for leading each of the seven sessions, as well as ideas for ways to plan and implement the *ReConnecting* experience in your particular setting. You may make copies of the guide for multiple leaders.

Publicity and Poster

Materials have been included to help you publicize the *ReConnecting* experience for your congregation. Several different sizes and formats of a *ReConnecting* poster can be found on the DVD. Display these posters throughout your church to advertise when and where you will be offering the program. We have given you both an 8.5 x 11 size and a 11 x 17 size, in both PDF and TIFF format. If you have Acrobat© Reader, you can open a PDF version, print it out, and use a marker to fill in date, time, and location information on the bottom portion. Or you can open one of the TIFF files in a graphics program like Adobe© Photoshop or Photoshop Elements and type in this information. You will be able to print out the 8.5 x 11 version on a high quality color printer, or you can take the larger size to your local printshop for a printout.

The **Publicity** folder contains examples of a brochure, letters, and a registration card to help you inform your congregation about this exciting program. These files have been included as Microsoft Word documents and can be easily customized.

(Files included in the **Poster** folder are: **poster small.pdf, poster large.pdf, poster large.tif, poster small.tif;** the **Publicity** folder includes: **brochure.doc, registration card.doc, letter1.doc, letter2.doc**)

PowerPoint® Slideshows

Each session includes a short slideshow to help guide your group time. These slides are included as part of the DVD interface—and can be played directly from the session sub-menu—and also as PowerPoint files. If your church has the ability to connect a computer to a projector, you might prefer to copy the PowerPoint file to your hard drive and customize it for your particular setting. You would then be able to show it from PowerPoint just as you do with other presentations. (Files included: **Session1.ppt** through **Session7.ppt**.)

Acrobat Reader

The installation program for Adobe Acrobat Reader 5.05 has been included on the DVD so that you may easily install this program on your computer if you do not have it or if you have an older version that will not open the PDF files included. To install the reader, simply double-click the appropriate file for your computer platform and follow the onscreen instructions (**ar505enu.exe** for Windows; **ar505enu.bin** for Macintosh.)

HOW DO I ACCESS THESE RESOURCES?

To access the *Leader's Guide* and additional materials on the DVD, you will need to place it in a computer DVD-ROM drive. To browse to these data folders in Windows, open **Windows Explorer** and find the *ReConnecting* disk icon. Double-click the DVD icon for a listing of the contents. (Be patient; it may take several seconds for the list to appear.) You may also use **My Computer** to get a listing of the data folders. However, you will probably need to right-click the DVD icon and choose **Explore** rather than double-clicking since this might cause the DVD to begin playing. On a Macintosh, simply double-click the *ReConnecting* DVD icon to view the contents of the disk.

Once you have located the file you need, either copy the file to your hard drive or double-click the file to open it from the disk. If you open the file from the disk, remember that manipulating the file this way may be slower than if you copy it to your hard drive.

PLAYING THE DVD ON A SET-TOP PLAYER

Set-top DVD players are connected to a TV. If you have played a DVD motion picture previously, you will see that the *ReConnecting* DVD behaves in the same way. Once inserted, the disk will begin playing automatically and will first bring up the copyright screen, followed by the **Main** menu. To navigate through the DVD menus, use the **Up** and **Down** arrow keys on your remote to move the pointer to the menu item that you wish to play. After an item is highlighted, press **Play** to move to the next screen, advance a slide, or to begin playing an item such as a video, music, or a presentation slideshow. Clicking the **Title** button will take you to back to the very beginning of the disk.

Volume is also adjusted in the normal way for your DVD player. Other buttons on the remote, like **Fast Forward**, will allow you to quickly move through a video or jump to the next item on the screen.

DVD Player Navigation Tips:

Title/Top=Beginning or Root Menu

Menu=Up one level

Arrow Keys=Move through graphical navigation buttons

Forward/Reverse=Fast forward or rewind video or music track

Next/Previous/Skip= Advance through slides

Stop=Restart DVD

Play=Play video, music or slideshow; advance slide

RECOMMENDED SYSTEM REQUIREMENTS FOR WINDOWS:

- Windows 98 and higher (ME or higher recommended)
- At least 400 MHz processor; 600 or higher
- 64 MB of memory; 128 or 256 recommended.
- DVD drive with appropriate drivers and software

RECOMMENDED SYSTEM REQUIREMENTS FOR MACINTOSH:

- G3 processor; 350 Mhz
- OS 9 or higher
- At least 64 MB of memory; 128 or 256 recommended.
- DVD drive with appropriate drivers and software

Computer Navigation Tips:

Title/Top=Beginning or Root Menu

Menu=Up one level

   Title=Back to Root

   Root=Back to Root or previous menu

   Subtitle=Back to previous menu

Return=Stop playing Centering music

Arrow Keys=Move through graphical navigation buttons

Forward/Reverse=Fast forward or rewind video or music track

Next/Previous=Advance through slides

Stop=Exit DVD

Each slideshow also contains the music for that session and will automatically begin playing the music once you reach the slide with the music credits on it. Sessions 4, 6, and 7 also include the lyrics to the song and the slides will automatically advance in sync with the music. To stop the music and return to the menu, simply highlight the **Play Centering Music** button again and click **Play.**

This particular DVD contains content on both sides. **Sessions One through Three** are located on **Side 1** and **Sessions Four through Seven** are located on **Side 2**. If you try to access one of the sessions from the session menu that is not located on the current side, a screen will appear that instructs you to eject the DVD from the player, turn it over, and begin playing again. (The DVD is labeled on the inner metallic ring.)

Many of the screens also have embedded graphical buttons, such as **Menu**, to help you navigate. Selecting the graphical **Menu** button will take you back one level in the menu structure, depending on where you are. For example, if you have the menu for Session One onscreen, selecting **Menu** will take you back to the main session menu, which lists all seven sessions. Selecting the **Back** or **Next** button will move you through the menus at the same level, which in this example are the individual session menus.

USING THE **DVD** ON A COMPUTER

If you have the capability to hook a computer with a DVD player to a projector, you may choose to use this method to display the video and music components for the sessions. Every computer will have a different type of proprietary software that comes with the DVD drive, and the controls on each will vary slightly. Many of the buttons on the software interface will act just like the buttons on a DVD remote, though there will be some variation. Using the up and down arrow buttons on your software remote will cycle through highlighting each of the buttons, functioning just as they do on a set-top DVD player. (**Up** and **Left** will move through the buttons clockwise; **Down** and **Right**=counter-clockwise.) Once you have highlighted the button you want, hit the **Enter** key to activate the button. The advantage, however, of the computer navigation over the DVD set-top player is your ability to use the mouse to easily select the item you want by clicking on it.

In general, clicking the **Menu** button will take you back one step: if you are simply in a menu, it will take you up one level to the previous one; if you are playing a video, it will stop the video and take you back to the Session sub-menu. You can also use the **Menu** button to exit out of a video or slideshow. Depending on where you are, you may have several choices when you click the **Menu** button. **Title** takes you back to the very beginning; **Root** takes you back to the previous menu (if this is your only other choice); or if you also have **Subtitle** as a choice, **Root** will take you back to the opening **Main** menu while **Subtitle** will take you back to the previous menu (usually the individual session menu).

Clicking the **Title** button will take you to back to the very beginning of the disk. The **Fast Forward** and **Rewind** buttons will allow you to advance or rewind the video. **Next** and **Previous** will only work to advance you through the slides in the slideshow.

Each slideshow also contains the music for that session and will automatically begin playing it once you reach the slide with the music credits on it. Sessions 4, 6, and 7 also include the lyrics to the song and the slides will automatically advance with the music. To stop the music and advance, you can simply click the **Next** button in Sessions 1, 2, 3, and 5 or **Menu > Root** in Sessions 4, 6, and 7.

Recommended Resources on Wesley

John Wesley on Christian Beliefs: The Standard Sermons in Modern English Vol. 1, 1-20, Kenneth Cain Kinghorn. ISBN 0-687-05296-3, $28.00.

John Wesley on the Sermon on the Mount: The Standard Sermons in Modern English Vol. 2, 21-33, Kenneth Cain Kinghorn. ISBN 0-687-02810-8, $28.00.

John Wesley: Holiness of Heart and Life, Charles Yrigoyen. ISBN 0-687-05686-1, $11.00.

Responsible Grace, Randy Maddox. ISBN 0-68700334-2, $24.00.

The Scripture Way of Salvation: The heart of Wesley's Theology, Kenneth J. Collins. ISBN 0-687-00962-6, $20.00.

Practical Divinity Volume 1: Theology in the Wesleyan Tradition, Thomas Langford. ISBN 0-687-07382-0, $25.00.

Practical Divinity Volume 2: Readings in Wesleyan Theology, Thomas Langford. ISBN 0-687-01247-3, $25.00.

A Wesleyan Spiritual Reader, Rueben P. Job. ISBN 0-687-05701-9, $15.00.

Rethinking Wesley's Theology for Contemporary Methodism, Randy Maddox. ISBN 0-687-06045-1, $24.00.

Wesley and the Quadrilateral: Renewing the Conversation, Stephen Gunter, Scott Jones, Ted Campbell, Rebekah Miles, Randy Maddox. ISBN 0-687-06055-9, $20.00.

A Real Christian: The Life of John Wesley, Kenneth J. Collins. ISBN 0-687-08246-3, $20.00.

Conversion in the Wesleyan Tradition, Kenneth J. Collins, John Tyson. ISBN 0-687-09107-1, $27.00.

The Wesleyan Tradition: A Paradigm for Renewal, Paul Chilcote. ISBN 0-687-09563-8, $24.00.

The New Creation: John Wesley's Theology Today, Theodore Runyon. ISBN 0-687-09602-2, $21.00.

John Wesley's Conception and Use of Scripture, Scott Jones. ISBN 0-687-20466-6, $20.00.

Wesley and the People Called Methodists, Richard Heitzenrater. ISBN 0-687-44311-3, $24.00.

The Works of John Wesley, Volume 24, W. Reginald Ward and Richard Heitzenrater, eds. ISBN 0-687-03349-7, $55.00.

John Wesley's Life and Ethics, Ronald H. Stone. ISBN 0-687-05632-2, $25.00.

Aldersgate Reconsidered, Randy Maddox. ISBN 0-687-00984-7, $17.00.

John Wesley's Sermons: An Anthology, Albert C. Outler. ISBN 0-687-20495-X, $22.00.

JW and Company. ISBN 0-687-81832-5, $79.95.

Happy Birthday, John Wesley. ISBN 0-687-51362-1, $6.50.

Visual Treasury of United Methodism. ISBN 0-687-72668-9, $17.00.

Hearts on Fire: The United Methodist Story, Student. ISBN 0-687-72796-0, $5.00.

Fired Up: Youth Living as United Methodists Today, Leader. ISBN 0-687-72797-9, $5.00.

Sermons and Hymns of John Wesley, Richard Heitzenrater. CD-ROM ISBN 0-687-03350-0, $47.20

The Works of John Wesley. CD-ROM ISBN 0-687-70922-1, $99.95.

Politcs in the Order of Salvation: Transforming Wesleyan Political Ethics, Theodore Weber. ISBN 0-687-316901, $35.00.

Endnotes

[1] Unless otherwise noted, quotations from Wesley were taken from *The Works of Wesley on CD-ROM* (Franklin: Providence House Publishers, 1995).

Additional Resources from Grace Community

RECONNECTING
A WESLEYAN GUIDE FOR THE RENEWAL OF OUR CONGREGATION

BY ROB WEBER

ReConnecting is a seven-week or seven-session experience designed to get congregational small groups in touch with historical (Wesleyan) roots and contemporary cultural forces, so that an individual can embrace his or her "priesthood." Also an envelope for a church vision and for strategic planning used throughout a congregation and based in prayer and identity formation. The use of the seven-session experience may be customized based on the churches' vision and need—to simulate a frozen congregation, to deploy as an adult group Lenten activity, or to revisit a Wesleyan heritage.

 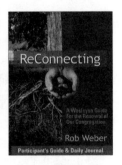

Leader's Guide	**Participant's Guide**
Publication Date: 10/2002	Publication Date: 10/2002
ISBN: 0-687-02234-7	ISBN: 0-687-06535-6
Price: $39.00	Price: $10.00

- Leader's Guide included on DVD as a PDF file (printed book contains text of the Participant's Guide)
- Promotional Video Trailer (a summary of the sessions).
- Customizable Poster (TIFF and PDF format)
- Publicity material (Sample letters, brochure, and registration card).

System Requirements:

DVD is compatible with all DVD set top players and most PC DVD-ROM players. **Participant's Guide does not include DVD.**

Note to Leaders:
You will want to purchase a copy of the Participant's Guide for each group member. You will also need to purchase at least one copy of the Leader's Guide with DVD.

VISUAL LEADERSHIP
THE CHURCH LEADER AS IMAGESMITH

BY ROB WEBER

Rob Weber stresses the importance for a church leader in our current multisensory and multi-cultural society to lead through engaging people in the multisensory world of images. This kind of leadership requires skills in storytelling and media.

Publication Date: 10/2002
ISBN: 0-687-07844-X
Price: $15.00

The leader must develop sensitivity to a variety of media forms as well as an understanding of the multiple levels of story, understanding, and image out of which (and into which) people live. This book examines the process of a "visual" form of leadership in which these principles and the process can be applied in a variety of settings by allowing for enhanced communication and fostering the development of congregational ownership over vision and direction.

REKINDLING
A GUIDE FOR CONGREGATIONS WITH MULTIPLE OR ALTERNATIVE WORSHIP PATTERNS

BY STACY HOOD

Whether your church is looking to add to a traditional music program or start a nontraditional music ministry, *ReKindling Your Music Ministry* provides worship leaders advice on making an effective transition into a new music format by reducing or better managing conflict. The "key" ingredient in a music ministry is to focus hearts on doing God's will—which is an excellent antidote to anxieties about entertainment and performance in worship.

$10 eBook available from Cokesbury.com in Palm, Abobe, and Microsoft formats. (Click "eBooks & eDocs" tab.)

For more information about Grace Community Church, visit www.gracehappens.org.
For more information about Rob Weber, visit www.RobWeber.org.

1 WHERE IN THE WORLD ARE WE?

Getting Our Bearings

How can you know where you're going if you don't know where you are?

—*Caterpillar,* **Alice's Adventures in Wonderland**

WHERE IN THE WORLD ARE WE?

Getting Our Bearings

In the film *Patch Adams*, Robin Williams portrays a man who seeks help from the medical profession for his problems. In the mental institution to which he has committed himself, his experience with the doctor is less than helpful; however, he does discover his own passion for helping people overcome their problems. To this end he decides to enter medical school and become a doctor, but what he finds at medical school is not at all what he expects. In the first lecture, he hears that the goal of medical school is to remove the humanity from the students so that they can be more than human, so that they can become doctors.

Throughout the movie, we see an unfolding of the struggle between Patch's desire to help people and the structure of the medical profession that has become depersonalized. Patch constantly ignores the rules of the profession in order to spend time with the patients, aid in the process of healing, and improve the quality of life. When the authorities ban him from using unconventional methods in his hospital work, he looks beyond the current system and moves beyond its boundaries to start a free medical clinic, the "Geshundheit Institute." Here, the dichotomy between patient and doctor is blurred. Doctors provide care for the patients, but the patients are all expected to share in the care of one another as well. Patient thus becomes doctor. Some of the authorities in the medical system who see Patch's unconventional approach to medicine as a threat to their power try to block him from graduation. After a hearing, Patch is told that, while his methods are unconventional and somewhat threatening to the current system, a fire burns within him, a flame of passion for the life of the patient that could spread "like a brushfire" throughout the medical profession.

The story of Patch Adams and his struggle with the medical profession is an analogy to the life of Jesus and his encounter with the religious system of his day. The Judaism of Jesus' day was developed as a system to provide connection between people and God. It was a system of rules and relationships designed to provide for a whole and healthy community. This was the system into which Jesus was born and in which he was recognized as a rabbi. Yet Jesus encountered challenges in the system when he attempted to focus on the needs of the people at the expense of systemic regulations. The Pharisees watched and criticized him for healing on the

Sabbath, eating with the unclean, spending time with tax collectors and prostitutes, and asking people to look beyond the law to the humanity for which it was created. Eventually, as Jesus moved further beyond the accepted systemic boundaries and as the threat to the authority of those in power became greater, Jesus, too, was brought to a hearing, but instead of recognizing his innovations and people-centered ministry as positive, he was sentenced to death.

In both these situations, systems created originally out of good motives evolved to the point of being concerned more with the maintenance of the system itself than with the purpose for which the system was created. The systems that had been created with the good of the people at heart had evolved to the point that the professional practitioners of the systems were the focus rather than the care receiver and his or her needs. In both cases, the reformer who turned the focus back to the original motivation for the system, and who bypassed the rules and regulations that had been created, was ridiculed and forced to operate outside the system. This recurrent pattern can be seen in the religious reformations in the Christian Church throughout history, and I believe that the phenomenon of institutionalization and renewal has much to say to us as we consider the challenges facing the church in the third millennium.

A Time of Changes and Choices

Here at the beginning of the twenty-first century, we are experiencing a time of rapid change. Ours is an exploding information age. It is a postmodern time, a time that many have labeled as post-Christian. The context of change provides many challenges and opportunities for the church. We are at a crossroads, a turning point in the life of the church. We cannot pretend that this is a time for life as usual. We cannot go about the business of doing simply what we are used to doing. We are in danger. During the 1950s the mainline church in America experienced tremendous growth. Over the past twenty-five years, that trend has reversed and the church has experienced a time of rapid decline. Various responses to the crisis of decline have emerged, ranging from denial to church growth strategies, to the charismatic renewal movement. It is in the context of turbulence, flux, and shifting social orientations that we must focus on the challenges facing the church in the twenty-first century.

WHERE IN THE WORLD ARE WE?

God's Words

Remember the days of old; consider the generations long past. Ask your father and he will tell you, your elders, and they will explain to you.

—Deuteronomy 32:7 (NIV)

Wesley's Words

The First general advice which one who loves your souls would earnestly recommend to every one of you is: "Consider, with deep and frequent attention, the peculiar circumstances wherein you stand."

—"Advice to the People Called Methodists"

Contemporary Words

DAY 1

A young man who was in the Marines shared with me an experience he had in "survival training." He said that he was "dropped" in a heavily wooded, mountainous area that was unfamiliar to him. All he was given was a compass and a topographical map. With these two items, he was directed to find his way to the rendezvous point. The first thing he had to do was attempt to discern where he was so that he could begin his journey. Without knowing where he was, it would be impossible for him to chart a course to his desired destination.

There are times when it is important for each of us as followers of Christ to stop and look carefully at where we are in the wilderness of life so that we can plot a course toward faithful life in Christ. This is also true for congregations. As we begin this *ReConnecting* process, let us consider where it is that we find ourselves as individuals and as a church so that we can embark on the continued journey toward faithfulness.

WEEK ONE

My Words

Thoughts tend to become "untangled" when we pause to write them down. Take a few moments and reflect. Ask God to show you a picture of where you are in your life of faith. Are you at the beginning of your journey? Are you in full sprint toward the fullness of life for which God has created you? Are you stalled along the road for one reason or another? Are you wandering around, uncertain as to your direction?

After reflecting on your life, write a short letter to God describing what you see.

WHERE IN THE WORLD ARE WE?

God's Words

I remember the days of long ago;
I meditate on all your works and consider what your hands have done.
I spread out my hands to you;
    my soul thirsts for you like a parched land.

—Psalm 143:5–6 (NIV)

Wesley's Words

Is it not the common practice of the old men to praise the past and condemn the present time? And this may probably operate much farther than one would at first imagine. When those that have more experience than us, and therefore we are apt to think more wisdom, are almost continually harping upon this, the degeneracy of the world; those who are accustomed from their infancy to hear how much better the world was formerly than it is now, (and so it really seemed to them when they were young, and just come into the world, and when the cheerfulness of youth gave a pleasing air to all that was round about them,) the idea of the world's being worse and worse would naturally grow up with them. And so it will be, till we, in our turn, grow peevish, fretful, discontented, and full of melancholy complaints, "How wicked the world is grown! How much better it was when we were young, in the golden days that we can remember!"

—"Of Former Times," no. 102, 9

DAY 2

Contemporary Words

Frequently, as I visit with leaders and members of churches, I hear stories about fond memories of the past, when the world didn't seem so fragmented, and the challenges facing the church didn't seem so complicated and difficult. I hear stories of full buildings and of vitality of ministry and mission. "I remember when we built this building. The church was full, and there were children and youth everywhere. People just don't seem to come to church like they used to. These days, people seem to be too busy and preoccupied. I wonder what has happened to commitment to the church."

Wesley heard these concerns as well. It was as if the people in the church were interpreting their present situation in light of their memories of what the church had been like before. The decline in participation and activity led to a sense of despair and backward focus. When life is lived with backward focus, it is difficult to appreciate the possibilities and opportunities that exist in the present. Wesley called people to stop idealizing the past, and to begin looking at the present with eyes toward the future. Could this be such a time for us as well?

—————— **WEEK ONE** ——————

My Words

What are some of the greatest changes in the world that you have experienced in your life?

How have those changes affected your life?

How have those changes affected the church?

WHERE IN THE WORLD ARE WE?

God's Words

Why do my people say, "We are free to roam; we will come to you no
    more"?
Does a maiden forget her jewelry, a bride her wedding ornaments?
Yet my people have forgotten me, days without number.

—Jeremiah 2:31–32 (NIV)

Wesley's Words

Was the last century more religious than this? In the former part of it, there was
much of the form of religion; and some undoubtedly experienced the power
thereof. But how soon did the fine gold become dim! How soon was it so min-
gled with worldly design, and with a total contempt both of truth, justice, and
mercy, as brought that scandal upon all religion which is hardly removed to this
day! Was there more true religion in the preceding century,—the age of the
Reformation? There was doubtless, in many countries, a considerable reformation of religious opinions; yea, and modes of worship, which were much
changed for the better, both in Germany and several other places. But it is well
known that Luther himself complained with his dying breath, "The people that
are called by my name (though I wish they were called by the name of Christ)
are reformed as to their opinions and modes of worship; but their tempers and
lives are the same as they were before."

—"Of Former Times," no. 102, 14

DAY 3

Contemporary Words

Travelers in Europe often visit a number of the great old cathedrals, the megachurches
of an earlier era. These cathedrals stand as a testimony to the commitment, faith, and
determination of those who spent their lives building them. The structures were built
in prominent locations in each city or town. The architecture served to point heav-
enward and provide a setting in which people could feel awe and reverence in the
presence of God. I notice, however, that many of these great buildings show little sign
of life, and feel like memorials to a previous age. In many places throughout Europe,
the church has experienced serious decline. What happened?

Some say that if you wonder about the future of the church in America, simply look
to what has happened in Europe.

WEEK ONE

My Words

Imagine your world without the influence of the Church. What would it be like?

Describe what that world would be like, paying attention to the feelings that accompany your description.

WHERE IN THE WORLD ARE WE?

God's Words

They devoted themselves to the apostles' teaching and to the fellowship, to the breaking of bread and to prayer. Everyone was filled with awe, and many wonders and miraculous signs were done by the apostles. All the believers were together and had everything in common. Selling their possessions and goods, they gave to anyone as he had need. Every day they continued to meet together in the temple courts. They broke bread in their homes and ate together with glad and sincere hearts, praising God and enjoying the favor of all the people. And the Lord added to their number daily those who were being saved.

—Acts 2:42–47 (NIV)

Wesley's Words

But between fifty and sixty years ago, a new phenomenon appeared in the world. Two or three young men, desiring to be scriptural Christians, met together for that purpose. Their number gradually increased. They were then all scattered. But fifty years ago, two of them met again; and a few plain people joined them, in order to help one another in the way to heaven. Since then they increased to many thousands, both in Europe and America. They are still increasing in number, and, as they humbly hope, in the knowledge and love of God; yea, and in what they neither hoped for nor desired, namely, in worldly substance.

—"Thoughts Upon a Late Phenomenon," no. 15

Contemporary Words

In the early 1700s, John Wesley embarked on a journey that changed the direction of the church. He emphasized a personal encounter with Christ and an experience of salvation. No longer was it enough to have a mental agreement with, or a belief in, Christianity. To be a Christian, one needed to be transformed into newness of life through a heart-felt relationship with the living Lord. The orientation of the church, which had become an institution maintained by and for the establishment, became directed towards those who were disenfranchised.

WEEK ONE

My Words

What is the difference between believing in Jesus and having a personal relationship with Jesus?

How do you experience salvation in your own life?

WHERE IN THE WORLD ARE WE?

God's Words

Forget the former things;
    do not dwell on the past.
See, I am doing a new thing!
Now it springs up; do you not perceive it?
I am making a way in the desert
    and streams in the wasteland.

—Isaiah 43:18–19 (NIV)

DAY 5

Wesley's Words

Yet God never left himself without witness. In every age, and in every nation, there were a few that truly feared God and wrought righteousness; and these were raised up, in their several generations, that they might be lights shining in a benighted world. But few of them answered the design of Providence for any considerable time. In every age, most of the excellent ones of the earth, being weary of the contradiction of sinners, separated from them, and retired, if not into deserts, yet into distinct churches or religious bodies. So their light no longer shone among men, among those that needed them most; but they contentedly gave up the world to the service of its old master.

—"Thoughts Upon a Late Phenomenon," no. 3

Contemporary Words

Wesley's objective was "To reform the world and to spread scriptural holiness across the land." The movement that he started had a great and powerful effect on England and the budding nation in America. Over the years, Methodists have accomplished much as they sought to bring the touch of Christ to the lost and the disenfranchised. Wesley noticed, however, that in many instances, churches had become focused inward rather than outward so that the majority of the activities of the church were devoted to self-preservation rather than the original mission. This pattern is a natural pattern of institutional development, but unless the move toward inward focus is countered by a re-focusing on the original mission, then the institution will decline until it no longer exists.

WEEK ONE

My Words

Why does the church exist?

In the form of a letter, describe to God the main areas of mission and activity of your congregation.

NOTES

2 COMING HOME

Rediscovering the Roots Of the Methodist Movement

Therefore I intend to keep on reminding you of these things, though you know them already and are established in the truth that has come to you.

—2 Peter 1:12 (NRSV)

COMING HOME

Rediscovering the Roots of the Methodist Movement

I remember hearing someone tell about a family who had a son come home from Vietnam. It was a time of preparation and joy because he was returning and had not been killed. It was also an awkward time because while he was coming home and seemed in every way to be healthy and whole, just as when he had left, he had developed amnesia. He was coming home to the place of his childhood, yet he could not remember that childhood. He would come home to look into the faces of his mother, father, sisters, and brothers and know that at one time in his life they had been close, yet now, he didn't know who they were. The family knew that this was going to be a difficult time, but they also knew how important it is to be connected to family and memory. They decided to find everything they could that might help him relearn his family identity, his history, his memory.

Many of us may be in a similar situation when it comes to memories of the history and heritage of our faith. We haven't necessarily been "off to war," although some have, but we have been off in a "foreign land" of a rapidly changing culture. This week begins that process of *ReConnecting* with memory so that we will feel at home in our family of faith once again. As we look back, we will tap into a time wherein Wesley had the opportunity to share with his "flock" a "Readers' Digest version" of the history the people called Methodists.

On April 21, 1777, the foundation of Wesley's new church facility in London was being laid. On this occasion Wesley took time to reflect on the events that shaped the movement that became the Methodist Church. This week, we will use those reflections and remembering as the basis for our readings.

As we reconnect to the story of John Wesley, which is our own story and a part of our corporate memory, I believe that we, too, can capture a sense of that powerful faith and that passionate calling. I believe that it is possible for us to get a sense of the vision that drove Wesley to make disciples and to see scriptural holiness spread across the face of the earth. I also believe that if we allow ourselves to seek with open hearts and minds, the presence of God can and will be made powerfully real to us.

Over the next few weeks, we will look more deeply into some of the experiences, events, and outcomes of the process of living out this newfound faith and direction and the way these experiences shaped the church that has shaped us.

John Wesley's Formative Experiences

1) Family of Faith: He was raised by parents who understood the importance of the life of faith, and in this setting he was able to witness not only the message of the importance of faith but also faith and personal devotion lived out on a daily basis.

2) Hand of God: He had an experience of God's touch on his life and believed that in some way he had been set apart by God for a purpose. He was a "brand plucked from the burning."

3) Continuing Formation: He had a commitment to education and the practice of the spiritual disciplines and to being part of a mutual accountability group.

4) Life of Service: His faith was developed by and expressed in works of service and outreach.

5) Experience of Failure: He knew firsthand the experience of failure and the importance of trusting in God's grace. This allowed him to maintain an openness to new ideas and remain careful so as not to become so dogmatic that he could not change his mind.

6) Experience of Faith: His life was changed when his faith became experienced instead of just believed.

7) Reaching Out: His life and ministry became driven by the motion and direction found in living out the Great Commission.

COMING HOME

God's Words

Is not this man a brand plucked from the fire?

—Zechariah 3:2b (NRSV)

Wesley's Words

"Saved from the Fire"

Seeing the room was very light, I called to the maid to take me up. But none answering, I put my head out of the curtains, and saw streaks of fire on the top of the room. I got up and ran to the door, but could get no farther, all the floor beyond it being in a blaze. I then climbed up on a chest which stood near the window: One in the yard saw me, and proposed running to fetch a ladder. Another answered, "There will not be time; but I have thought of another expedient: Here, I will fix myself against the wall; lift a light man, and set him on my shoulders." They did so, and he took me out of the window. Just then the whole roof fell in; but it fell inward, or we had been all crushed at once. When they brought me into the house where my father was, he cried out, "Come, neighbours, let us kneel down! Let us give thanks to God! He has given me all my eight children: Let the house go; I am rich enough."

—From John Wesley's account of the Epworth fire on August 24, 1709[1]

Contemporary Words

This early experience of John Wesley has become part of the "Wesley legend." It has been told often and embellished in many ways. Was it an event that demonstrated that he was specially chosen by God? That is a possibility; however, I believe that through this story, we are reminded of a more fundamental truth. If that one person had decided to run off and get the ladder to save the young John, he would have never been more than the young John. The world would never have heard of John Wesley. The truth is that our lives are fragile. They are the only opportunity we have to live with passion and purpose...and, like Wesley, to make a mark upon the world.

DAY 1

WEEK TWO

My Words

How are you living TODAY—so as to make the gift of your life all that God has created it to be?

List some of the dreams you believe God might have for you.

Write about one step you could make today to move closer to one of those dreams.

COMING HOME

God's Words

They devoted themselves to the apostles' teaching and fellowship,
to the breaking of bread and to prayer.

—Acts 2:42 (NIV)

Wesley's Words

"The Birth of the Movement"

We may consider, First, the rise and progress of this work:...As to the rise of it. In the year 1725, a young student at Oxford was much affected by reading Kempis's "Christian Pattern," and Bishop Taylor's "Rules of Holy Living and Dying." He found an earnest desire to live according to those rules, and to flee from the wrath to come. He sought for some that would be his companions in the way, but could find none; so that, for several years, he was constrained to travel alone, having no man either to guide or to help him. But in the year 1729, he found one who had the same desire. They then endeavoured to help each other; and, in the close of the year, were joined by two more. They soon agreed to spend two or three hours together every Sunday evening. Afterwards they sat two evenings together, and, in a while, six evenings, in the week; spending that time in reading the Scriptures, and provoking one another to love and to good works.

—"On Laying the Foundation of a New Chapel," no. 132, 1.1

Contemporary Words

What was it that enabled Wesley to become such a leader? In the above passage, we can see some of the important pieces of his spiritual formation.

- He spent time in spiritual reading.

- He had an earnest desire to know God's will for his life and a willingness to live it even if it meant being alone.

- He actively sought companions to share the journey.

- He put himself in a situation wherein he was held accountable for his spiritual integrity by the scriptures and his companions.

DAY 2

—————————— WEEK TWO ——————————

My Words

How can this model of Wesley's early spiritual discipline shape your life as you seek a deeper connection with God?

<u>**Reading Spiritual Works**</u>

<u>**Seeking God's Will for My Life**</u>

<u>**Finding Spiritual Companions**</u>

<u>**Keeping Accountable**</u>

COMING HOME

God's Words

Then Barnabas went to Tarsus to look for Saul, and when he had found him, he brought him to Antioch. So it was that for an entire year they met with the church and taught a great many people, and it was in Antioch that the disciples were first called "Christians."

—Acts 11:25–26 (NRSV)

Wesley's Words

"From Whence the Name"

The regularity of their behaviour gave occasion to a young gentleman of the College to say, "I think we have got a new set of *Methodists*,"—alluding to a set of Physicians, who began to flourish at Rome about the time of Nero, and continued for several ages. The name was new and quaint; it clave to them immediately; and from that time, both those four young gentlemen, and all that had any religious connexion with them, were distinguished by the name of *Methodists*.

—"On Laying the Foundation of a New Chapel," no. 132, 1.2

DAY 3

Contemporary Words

In Antioch, the group under the teaching of Barmabas and Paul came to be known as Christians because they were followers of Christ. Another interpretation of the name is "little Christs." These people didn't choose the name. They didn't sit down and have a "let's name the group" session. People observed their life together and called them Christians.

The name Methodist was originally used as a derogatory term. People looked at the careful seriousness with which the young students practiced their faith and gave them the name "Methodists."

My Words

By what name would you be called as a result of observing the way you live out your spiritual life?

Write a description of some of the most important dimensions of your spiritual life.

By what name would you *like* to be called, and why?

COMING HOME

God's Words

Let no evil talk come out of your mouths, but only what is useful for building up, as there is need, so that your words may give grace to those who hear. And do not grieve the Holy Spirit of God, with which you were marked with a seal for the day of redemption. Put away from you all bitterness and wrath and anger and wrangling and slander, together with all malice, and be kind to one another, tenderhearted, forgiving one another, as God in Christ has forgiven you. Therefore be imitators of God, as beloved children, and live in love, as Christ loved us and gave himself up for us, a fragrant offering and sacrifice to God.

—Ephesians 4:29–5:2 (NRSV)

Wesley's Words

"Looking for Salvation by Following the Rules"

DAY 4

In the four or five years following, another and another were added to the number, till, in the year 1735, there were fourteen of them who constantly met together. Three of these were Tutors in their several Colleges; the rest, Bachelors of Arts or Under-graduates. They were all precisely of one judgment, as well as of one soul; all tenacious of order to the last degree, and observant, for conscience' sake, of every rule of the Church, and every statute both of the University and of their respective Colleges. They were all orthodox in every point; firmly believing not only the Three Creeds, but whatsoever they judged to be the doctrine of the Church of England, as contained in her Articles and Homilies. As to that practice of the Apostolic Church, (which continued till the time of Tertullian, at least in many Churches,) the having all things in common, they had no rule, nor any formed design concerning it; but it was so in effect, and it could not be otherwise; for none could want anything that another could spare. This was the infancy of the work. They had no conception of anything that would follow. Indeed, they took "no thought for the morrow," desiring only to live to-day.

—"On Laying the Foundation of a New Chapel," no. 132, 1.3

Contemporary Words

Passionate sincerity characterized these young "Methodists." With all their hearts, souls, and minds they pursued the fulfillment of the work of God in their lives. They drew on two sources for their pattern of behavior: the teachings and rules of the Church of England and their understanding of the practices of the early church. Both of these sources came from the well of church tradition. In the tradition of the Church, we find a record of the work of faithful generations who have gone before. It is a resource for us as we strive to live out our faith today.

—————— **WEEK TWO** ——————

My Words

What are some of the church traditions that are most important to you and why?

Traditions of the Church Year

Traditions in Worship

COMING HOME

God's Words

Remember the long way that the LORD your God has led you these forty years in the wilderness, in order to humble you, testing you to know what was in your heart, whether or not you would keep his commandments. He humbled you by letting you hunger, then by feeding you with manna, with which neither you nor your ancestors were acquainted, in order to make you understand that one does not live by bread alone, but by every word that comes from the mouth of the LORD.

—Deuteronomy 8:2–3 (NRSV)

Wesley's Words

"The Trip to Georgia (accompanied by the rules)"

Many imagined that little society would be dispersed, and Methodism (so called) come to an end, when, in October, 1735, my brother, Mr. Ingham, and I, were induced, by a strange chain of providences, to go over to the new colony in Georgia. Our design was to preach to the Indian nations bordering upon that province; but we were detained at Savannah and Frederica, by the importunity of the people, who, having no other Ministers, earnestly requested that we would not leave them. After a time, I desired the most serious of them to meet me once or twice a week at my house. Here were the rudiments of a Methodist society; but, notwithstanding this, both my brother and I were as vehemently attached to the Church as ever, and to every rubric of it; insomuch that I would never admit a Dissenter to the Lord's Supper, unless he would be re-baptized. Nay, when the Lutheran Minister of the Saltzburghers at Ebenezer, being at Savannah, desired to receive it, I told him, I did not dare to administer it to him, because I looked upon him as unbaptized; as I judged baptism by laymen to be invalid: And such I counted all that were not episcopally ordained.

—"On Laying the Foundation of a New Chapel," no. 132, 1.4

Contemporary Words

For all his piety and practice, powerful knowledge of the Bible, as well as adherence to Christian traditions, Wesley didn't do too well on his missionary journey to Georgia. He was so dedicated to the laws of the church and his own way of living out those laws (rules) that he was blinded to the needs and differences of those around him. His unwavering commitment to upholding the rules of the tradition became a stumbling block for him and his ministry.

DAY 5

WEEK TWO

My Words

Can you think of a time in which you have been so committed to "the way it has always been done before" that you might have missed something God was trying to tell you, or missed reaching someone God wanted to touch through you?

Write briefly about this experience.

Endnotes

[1] Richard Heitzenriter, *The Elusive Mr. Wesley, Vol. 1* (Nashville: Abingdon Press, 1984), p. 36.

3 GOING DEEP

Discovering the Roots Of Authentic Spirituality

"Earth's crammed with Heaven,
and every common bush afire with God;
But only he who sees takes off his shoes -
The rest sit round it and pluck blackberries . . ."

—*"Aurora Leigh," Bk. 7, line 820*
Elizabeth Barrett Browning

Session **3**

GOING DEEP

Discovering the Roots of Authentic Spirituality

I knew I should have checked it sooner, but I had been so busy with getting ready for exams, then taking exams, then being glad that exams were over...Then, of course, I had to begin filling the 1966 VW bug full of laundry, and the drum set, and the albums (those were like big black plastic CDs that you couldn't play in the car) and the plants I couldn't leave in the dorm over the winter break. By the time I'd finished packing the car, it was probably too late to leave, but the dorms were closed, and I wanted to get home. "I can make it," I thought. "All I need is coffee." Five hundred miles through the middle of the night, already experiencing post-finals sleep deprivation syndrome—"No problem!" My reasoning was somewhat obscured by the pseudo invulnerability that comes from being nineteen. "I can do anything," I thought.

The moon was bright that night and stars filled the deep Southern sky. Now, here it was, well after midnight, somewhere along the highway in a very rural part of Mississippi (or was it Alabama?), and I noticed it. The needle in the only gauge, other than the speedometer, on the light blue metal dashboard was resting on the side of the gauge, just to the left of "E." Well, being the well-educated young man I was, I tapped the glass wondering why it was resting off to the side like that. Then a sudden realization of the problem swept over me: "It does that when there is no gas in the tank, which must mean . . ."

Just a few hours before, I had imagined I was invincible. I could take on anything. Now, I was alone in the middle of nowhere, in the middle of the night, in my little 1966 VW bug, just hoping I could make it to the next exit. Suddenly, the world seemed so much bigger and I felt so much smaller. The miles seemed longer than before. The fear of being stuck "out there" without any way to contact anyone increased (how used to cell phones I've become). I thought about the gas stations I'd passed on the way out of town. I remembered times when the tank had been full. I wondered what would happen if I poured the bottle of "Old Spice" aftershave in the gas tank. I tried to "will" the needle back to the right, but it was no use. First, a little cough, then a chug, small enough to almost believe that it was really nothing. Then a definite sputter. Then the sound of the engine stopped all together. The power driving the car, that I had somehow mistakenly assumed was my own power, ran out. For a while the car continued forward on its own. Rolling down the road in the moonlight in a landscape that had suddenly become strangely silent. I steered toward the shoulder. The gravel crunched beneath the tires until the car came to a stop. Then silence.

The experience of being forced to stop made it possible for me to see past the illusion of my own power to the need of a power beyond myself, and it helped me to realize that if you don't keep gas in the car on a regular basis, you will eventually encounter a situation wherein you need it, but there is nothing you can do about it on your own.

Up until that point, the evening had been filled with the sound and vibration that comes only from a '66 bug with a metal interior. It was a sound to which I had become accustomed. It was a sound that, along with maintaining my illusion of control and power, drowned out the songs of the fall leaves rustling in the trees and the cicadas singing in the recently stubbled cotton field.

I got out and walked around. I looked at the car. It still looked just like the thing that only a moment before had been propelling me forward through the night with power and purpose. Now it was empty. It had the form but not the power. It wasn't the car's fault. It got great mileage, but you still had to put gas in it. I'd been too busy to stop and look at the gas gauge.

Wesley's Concern

Wesley wrote, "I am not concerned that the people called Methodists should ever cease to exist, either in Europe or in America, but that they would continue to exist only as a dead sect, having the form of religion without the power." This week we will look at some of the reasons Wesley thought the church was not thriving as it could and see if those words speak to our own situation as individuals and as a church.

Spiritual Oat Bran or Mall Walking

The "means of grace" are not what give us a meaningful spiritual life. Life in and with God is a gift of grace. The "means of grace" are the practices that make it more able for us to allow God into our lives. Each day we will explore one of the "means of grace" during the reading and reflection time. Even if these activities seem uncomfortable at first, don't give up. Some of you may know what it is to restart or intensify an exercise program or a diet. It is less than comfortable, but if you stick with it, you will see great benefit.

This week, you have before you a "sampler" of some different types of spiritual exercises. Take your time and try to see which of these exercises might benefit you most.

GOING DEEP

God's Words

...holding to the outward form of godliness but denying its power. Avoid them!

—2 Timothy 3:5 (NRSV)

Wesley's Words

"What Makes a Christian?"

In these [places], every branch of Christianity is openly and largely declared; and thousands upon thousands continually hear and receive "the truth as it is in Jesus." Why is it then, that even in these parts Christianity has had so little effect? Why are the generality of the people, in all these places, Heathens still? no better than the Heathens of Africa or America, either in their tempers or in their lives? Now, how is this to be accounted for? I conceive, thus: It was a common saying among the Christians in the primitive Church, "The soul and the body make a man; the spirit and discipline make a Christian;" implying, that none could be real Christians, without the help of Christian discipline. But if this be so, is it any wonder that we find so few Christians; for where is Christian discipline? In what part of England (to go no farther) is Christian discipline added to Christian doctrine? Now, whatever doctrine is preached, where there is not discipline, it cannot have its full effect upon the hearers.

—"Causes of the Inefficacy of Christianity," no. 116, 7

Contemporary Words

In this sermon, Wesley is reflecting on the lack of effect that Christianity was having on the world of his day. There were plenty of churches and many people who gathered in them, but poverty, abuse, inhumane conditions, and the lack of education continued to be widespread. Christianity seemed common as a belief, but those who were believers seemed much the same as those who were not. There was much invested in the religion of the day. The church was powerful, the buildings were magnificent, yet the fact that there were Christians living in the world didn't seem to make much of a difference to the surrounding society. Why was that? The cause, says Wesley, is the lack of connection to the Spirit and Christian discipline. The Church without connection to the Spirit is like the '66 VW Bug without any gas—it has the form, but not the power. We can move toward reconnection by intentionally seeking a living and growing relationship through Christian discipline—regular participation in the "means of grace."

WEEK THREE

My Words

Practice being in the Presence of God. On this first day of reading and reflection this week, we will focus on drawing near to God and deepening the living relationship for which we were created. I invite you to take a little time and do something that will set your study or prayer place apart as a sacred place where you go to meet with God. Whether at home in a quiet place or on your lunch break in a busy office, you can do some simple things to remind yourself of the sacred nature of what you are doing.

Set up your space. Keep your Bible in the place where you will go to study and to pray. When you are finished with one day's reading, go ahead and open the Bible to the next day's reading and leave it there. Then it will be open and waiting for you, inviting you to return. You may want to keep a picture, or a cross, or an item in your space that helps you remember a time when you felt particularly close to God. One of the simplest and most effective things to do is to light a candle to remind yourself that Jesus said, "I am the light of the world." As you read, reflect, study and pray, while the candle is burning, you are reminded of the nearness of Christ.

Take a few moments to become quiet. Be open. Ask God to help you draw near. Wait... Take time to reflect on some of the experiences in your own life, big or small, looking for one wherein you can remember having sensed the presence of God.

Write what you remember of that experience.

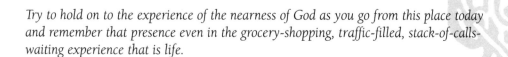

Try to hold on to the experience of the nearness of God as you go from this place today and remember that presence even in the grocery-shopping, traffic-filled, stack-of-calls-waiting experience that is life.

GOING DEEP

God's Words

Then he said to them all, "If any want to become my followers, let them deny themselves and take up their cross daily and follow me."

—Luke 9:23 (NRSV)

Wesley's Words

"The Missing Ingredient"

But to return to the main question. Why has Christianity done so little good, even among us? among the Methodists,—among them that hear and receive the whole Christian doctrine, and that have Christian discipline added thereto, in the most essential parts of it? Plainly, because we have forgot, or at least not duly attended to, those solemn words of our Lord, "If any man will come after me, let him deny himself, and take up his cross daily, and follow me." It was the remark of a holy man, several years ago, "Never was there before a people in the Christian Church, who had so much of the power of God among them, with so little self-denial." Indeed the work of God does go on, and in a surprising manner, notwithstanding this capital defect; but it cannot go on in the same degree as it otherwise would; neither can the word of God have its full effect, unless the hearers of it "deny themselves, and take up their cross daily."

—"The Inefficacy of Christianity," no. 116, 13

Contemporary Words

Wesley's call to prayer is expected even in the midst of a hectic and demanding schedule:

"The reformers were probably almost as busy as we, yet their response to the daily grind was an inversion of our values and attitudes. And so Luther said, 'I'm so busy and burdened with these mounting responsibilities that unless I pray four hours a day I won't get all of my work done.' Later John Wesley wrote to the pastor of a small congregation who complained that Wesley was expecting too much by way of study and prayer: 'Oh, begin! Set some time each day for prayer and Scripture whether you like it or not. It is for your life! Else you will be a trifler all your days.'"

—Norman Shawchuck and Gustave Rath, *Benchmarks of Quality in the Church*, p. 15.[1]

Week Three

My Words

Deepening the Experience of Formal Prayers

One of the complaints against written liturgy and formal, oft-repeated prayers is that they soon are memorized and become little more than a recitation of words without the heart, soul, or mind ever getting into the experience. As one who loves to spend time at the monastery I know the value of the printed liturgy and the presence of God in the prepared word. I do agree, however, that if we are not careful, we can fall into the habit of simply reading without being engaged by the words. One simple exercise to keep the words of ancient prayers and liturgies fresh is paraphrasing, or putting the writing into your own words. Today we will try it with the familiar passage, the Lord's Prayer.

Our Father, who art in Heaven, Hallowed be thy name.

Thy Kingdom come, Thy will be done, on Earth as it is in Heaven.

Give us this day our daily bread, and forgive us our trespasses as we forgive those who trespass against us.

Lead us not into temptation, but deliver us from evil, for thine is the Kingdom and the power and the glory, forever. Amen.

GOING DEEP

God's Words

Command those who are rich in this present world not to be arrogant nor to put their hope in wealth, which is so uncertain, but to put their hope in God, who richly provides us with everything for our enjoyment. Command them to do good, to be rich in good deeds, and to be generous and willing to share. In this way they will lay up treasure for themselves as a firm foundation for the coming age, so that they may take hold of the life that is truly life.

—1 Timothy 6:17–19 (NIV)

Wesley's Words

"Learning the Secret of Stewardship"

Why is not the spiritual health of the people called Methodists recovered?... O why do not we, that have all possible helps, "walk as Christ also walked?" Hath he not left us an example that we might tread in his steps? But do we regard either his example or precept? To instance only in one point: Who regards those solemn words, "Lay not up for yourselves treasures upon earth?" Of the three rules which are laid down on this head, in the sermon on "The Mammon of Unrighteousness," you may find many that observe the First rule, namely, "Gain all you can." You may find a few that observe the Second, "Save all you can:" But how many have you found that observe the Third rule, "Give all you can?"

—"Causes of the Inefficacy of Christianity," no. 116, 8

DAY 3

Contemporary Words

Why is the church not as alive as it could be and as alive as we would want it to be if we had invited Jesus to lunch? The reason is the lack of surrender. We tend to try to hold on to control. We want to be in control of the way things happen in church, in our financial lives, and even in our relationships. I find it much easier to say, "Not what you want, Lord, but what I want. Oh, and by the way, this is the way I'd like it." In his sermon, "On the Use of Money," Wesley said, "Earn all you can, save all you can, and give all you can." He knew that the practice of hard work, and careful saving coupled with a willingness to give freely and trust in God's provision aids in the development of compassionate and committed disciples, along with a church that has the resources to make a difference in the world. Many are good at earning, and some at saving, but missing is a passionate life of giving that demonstrates our hope in God and not in the wealth God enabled us to earn.

—————————— **WEEK THREE** ——————————

My Words

Ask and Reflect. Does my giving demonstrate:

- **My trust in God's providence rather than my wealth?**

- **My passionate commitment to the work of Christ through the church?**

- **My concern for the poor and the broken?**

- **What kind of gift would be sacrificial for me and honoring to God? What is something I could do specifically?**

GOING DEEP

God's Words

Woe to you, scribes and Pharisees, hypocrites! For you tithe mint, dill, and cummin, and have neglected the weightier matters of the law: justice and mercy and faith. It is these you ought to have practiced without neglecting the others. You blind guides! You strain out a gnat but swallow a camel!

Woe to you, scribes and Pharisees, hypocrites! For you clean the outside of the cup and of the plate, but inside they are full of greed and self-indulgence. You blind Pharisee! First clean the inside of the cup, so that the outside also may become clean.

—Matthew 23:23–26 (NRSV)

Wesley's Words

"There is No Power in the Means Themselves"

Secondly, before you use any means, let it be deeply impressed on your soul,—there is no *power* in this. It is, in itself, a poor, dead, empty thing: Separate from God, it is a dry leaf, it is a shadow. Neither is there any *merit* in my using this; nothing intrinsically pleasing to God; nothing whereby I deserve any favor at his hands, no, not a drop of water to cool my tongue. But, because God bids, therefore I do; because he directs me to wait in this way, therefore here I wait for his free mercy whereof cometh my salvation.

—"Means of Grace," no. 16, V. 4

Contemporary Words

One of the biggest misconceptions about spiritual exercises and religious rituals is that there is something intrinsically valuable about them, that if we just say prayers, or take communion, we somehow will be privileged by God. The other misconception is that liturgical practices and spiritual disciplines stand in the way of real and direct experience of God. Wesley had to struggle with arguments surrounding these misconceptions. On one side were the people deeply embedded in the traditional practices of the church who were afraid of the new movement toward spiritual renewal, with an emphasis on an experience of God. On the other side were those who were so committed to the immediate experience of God that they rejected any formal prayers or ritual as obstructions to an authentic spiritual life. Wesley, as he did in so many things, was able to see what was valuable in both sides. While he knew the value of a living relationship with a living God, he also knew the benefit of the practice of particular spiritual exercises. He is clear that these exercises are not the goal of the religious life, but are merely means to the end, which is a transformed and transforming life of discipleship.

— WEEK THREE —

My Words

* Materials needed for this session: a Bible, a cup (empty or filled with water or grape juice), some bread (a slice will do), and a picture or other representation of Jesus.

Holy Communion: I once had a conversation with a rabbi who had visited a church during a communion service. His fresh perspective helped me see two things. First, he reflected on what a powerful symbolic activity it was. It engaged the five senses of touch, taste, sight, sound, and smell. It carried with it a conceptual dimension and a spiritual expression. "What a beautiful and powerful thing, to be able to come to the altar together and take God inside of you." The other reflection was less flattering. After he had just expressed deep reverence for the sacrament and the depth of its meaning, he said, "It seems that most people are going up there as if it is just another task to do, like picking something up at the grocery store. If I had a sacrament like that, I would want to savor it and experience it to the fullest." It took an encounter with someone outside the church to help me understand how potentially powerful our own sacrament is.

Read Mark 14:22–25. Look at your picture or other representation of Jesus and think about the actual person there in that room talking to the disciples. Try to imagine what it looked like. **What were the sights and sounds? What were the smells? What were the feelings and emotions?**

Hold the bread. Imagine the hands of Jesus holding bread.

What does he mean when he says, "This is my body?"

How is he "broken for you?" What does that mean for you personally?

Hold the cup. **How is he "poured out for you?"**

Next time you participate in Holy Communion, allow these memories and images to surround you.

GOING DEEP

God's Words

"Now therefore revere the LORD, and serve him in sincerity and in faithfulness; put away the gods that your ancestors served beyond the River and in Egypt, and serve the LORD. Now if you are unwilling to serve the LORD, choose this day whom you will serve, whether the gods your ancestors served in the region beyond the River or the gods of the Amorites in whose land you are living; but as for me and my household, we will serve the LORD."

—Joshua 24:14–15 (NRSV)

Wesley's Words

"Becoming Like God"

I would earnestly advise you, Fourthly: "Keep in the very path wherein you now tread. Be true to your principles." Never rest again in the dead formality of religion. Pursue with your might inward and outward holiness; a steady imitation of Him you worship; a still increasing resemblance of his imitable perfections,—his justice, mercy, and truth.

—"Advice to the People Called Methodists"

DAY 5

Contemporary Words

Just before taking them across the river into the Promised Land, Joshua held up a choice before the people who would be making the journey. It wasn't a choice about what to believe. It was a choice about whether or not they would put away anything that competed for their total allegiance to God.

In his "Advice to the People Called Methodists," Wesley gives the same type of instruction. The life of a believer is not to be just the outer practices of attending a service or joining a particular congregation. The life of the believer is to be a life that seeks holiness, both inward and outward. It is to be a life that strives to grow closer to God in character and in relationship.

— WEEK THREE —

My Words

Think back over the week and some of the times of reflection you have had.

How are you becoming more aware of the deep places and the growing edges of your spiritual life?

Take a moment and be quiet in the presence of God. Listen. Wait. Just breathe and quiet your mind.

Write a letter to God about how you see your relationship, and where you want to grow closer. List two or three specific things that you can put into practice in the coming week that will help develop that process.

Dear God,

When you are finished writing, close your eyes and imagine offering the letter to God and staying there while God reads it.

How does God respond?

NOTES

Endnotes

[1] Norman Shawchuck and Gustave Rath, *Benchmarks of Quality in the Church* (Nashville: Abingdon Press, 1994) p. 15.

4 OUTSIDE THE GATES

Getting to Know the Cultures in Our Context

And so Jesus also suffered outside the city gate to make the people holy through his own blood.

—*Hebrews 13:12 (NIV)*

OUTSIDE THE GATES

Getting to Know the Cultures in Our Context

We heard him as we passed through the square before we went to dinner, and now as we made our way back toward the subway (or the "Tube," as it is called in London), we saw that he had not given up. In fact, the crowd had grown from a handful of onlookers to several dozen, all listening to the man who was singing for tips with an acoustic guitar and a battery-powered amp. The neon lights for the theatres and the "McDonald's" sign seemed somewhat out of place mounted on buildings that are several centuries old. The square was filled with people. All of them seemed to be headed somewhere. They moved at varying degrees of speed and with varying levels of purposeful intensity. Some of them looked as if they were headed to or from work, some to dinner or a show. A woman with face furrowed in anger walked quickly through the crowd while a slightly embarrassed and apologetic looking man hurried to catch up. Sightseeing parents with children tired from a day of exploration shuffled and tugged their way towards rest. It was a crossroads. It was a gathering place. It was a square filled with people from many different walks of life, different cultures, and even from different parts of the world.

The sounds, too, seemed to clutter the evening with their diversity—the roar of the double-decker buses moving an endless flood of people through Piccadilly Circus a couple of blocks over, the impatient blare of the horns of taxi drivers rushing to drop their human cargo while looking towards the next fare, the whistles of the police, the sirens of the emergency vehicles, the homeless man's request for spare change and the rattle of the pennies in his cup, the raucous voice of the drunk who was trying to get someone to dance with him, people speaking, or yelling, or laughing in a dozen different languages, all merging together into the constant cry of the ceaseless motion which is the city.

Then I heard something that changed the purpose of my listening. The sound I heard called me as a participant in the newly emerging melody of the familiar, a simple sound, the chords and the light picking of a song I remembered from high school. Something stirred within me, and I wanted to join with the guitar-playing leader of our spontaneous congregation. I couldn't help it. Suddenly, I found myself singing along like a youth at a bonfire. I was singing James Taylor's "You've Got a Friend." As I sang, I noticed that my wife was singing, too. With our arms around each other's waists, we sang. The music took center stage in the midst of the perpetual motion all around.

"You just call out my name,
And you know wherever I am,

I'll come running, to see you again...
...and I'll be there, yes I will.
You've got a friend."[1]

We sang as if that was what we had come there that evening to do, and as I looked around I saw that we weren't the only ones who had been carried into this moment of spontaneous song. The dozens who had paused to listen all seemed to be singing as well, and many more had stopped their frantic motion and had gathered around the shared melody. As I looked around the circle at the faces of those singing, I was moved even more deeply, for even though we were all singing in English, those whose voices were lifted were from India, Japan, the Middle East, different countries in Europe, America, and who knows how many other places. The singers were old and young; even the homeless man ceased the rattling of the cup and sang. For a moment the sound of the city had disappeared and there, in the middle of London, late at night, thousands of miles away from home, in the midst of a crowd of strangers from all over the world, I caught a glimpse of what it must have been like on the day of Pentecost.

Why was it that "You've Got a Friend" struck such a chord in the hearts of all of those people from all over the world? I think it was because the song touched a common human need or longing...the need to know that someone cares enough to come to us when we are hurting, or afraid, or alone. Wesley was called out beyond the walls of the to touch people who would have resonated with the feelings in that song. They were lost and alone. They were working as hard as they could, but couldn't make enough to get out of poverty. The children grew up in a world in which they saw parents with no education struggling day after day just to keep bread on the table. They had no opportunities for education, so they soon entered the poverty cycle. Many drank the cheap gin to escape the hopelessness of the situation and to dull the pain of deprivation.

It was to these people that the words of Wesley's preaching came and brought a message of real hope. The words came to remind them that there was someone who cared for them, not just for their souls in an afterlife that seemed, at times, too far away, but for them in the here and now. This was a message that was brought to the people outside the gates of the church in the 1700s.

What did it take?

At Pentecost, the noise of a people brought together for a celebration was transformed into the song of a people who were celebrating because they had been brought together. In the midst of diversity, a message emerged that spoke to the need in the heart of all who had gathered.

During the Wesleyan revival, the song swelled again:

"O for a thousand tongues to sing my great Redeemer's praise,
The glories of my God and King, the triumphs of His grace!"

What are the barriers to our moving outside the gates, or even opening the doors and welcoming those who are outside into our midst? What are the possibilities for ministry that await us?

And so Jesus also suffered outside the city gate to make the people holy through his own blood. Let us, then, go to him outside the camp, bearing the disgrace he bore. For here we do not have an enduring city, but we are looking for the city that is to come.

Through Jesus, therefore, let us continually offer to God a sacrifice of praise—the fruit of lips that confess his name. And do not forget to do good and to share with others, for with such sacrifices God is pleased.

Hebrews 13:12–16

OUTSIDE THE GATES

God's Words

Dear friends, since God so loved us, we also ought to love one another.

—1 John 4:11 (NIV)

Wesley's Words

"If we can't think alike, can't we still love alike?"

3. All men approve of this; but do all men practice it? Daily experience shows the contrary. Where are even the Christians who "love one another as He hath given us commandment?" How many hinderances lie in the way! The two grand, general hinderances are, First, that they cannot all think alike; and, in consequence of this, Secondly, they cannot all walk alike; but in several smaller points their practice must differ in proportion to the difference of their sentiments.

4. But although a difference in opinions or modes of worship may prevent an entire external union; yet need it prevent our union in affection? Though we cannot think alike, may we not love alike? May we not be of one heart, though we are not of one opinion? Without all doubt, we may. Herein all the children of God may unite, notwithstanding these smaller differences. These remaining as they are, they may forward one another in love and in good works.

—"The Catholic Spirit," no. 39, 3–4

DAY 1

Contemporary Words

Sometimes I drive through a section of the city in which I live that has obvious evidence of deep poverty. It is an area that is considered to be dangerous because of the frequency of violent crime. I reached over and pushed the auto lock button on the door as I sat at the traffic light. Then I looked up at the billboard above me. It was one of those plain black billboards with simple white writing. It said, "That love one another thing—I meant it. God"

I found myself in one of those rough and honest moments of self-examination in which I came up short of what I thought I believed. Maybe I do believe that I ought to love one another, just as God loves me. Maybe the problem is not so much in the right belief as it is in the right practice, or lack thereof. I wonder how my life would be different if I actually lived the command to love rather than just agreeing with it in my mind...?

WEEK FOUR

My Words

Can you remember a time in which you or someone very close to you was broken, far from God, in the midst of doing something wrong, or was otherwise difficult to love?

Try to think through some of the details of that situation and write them down. (*These will not be for sharing.*)

What was the nature of the hurt?

How was this person far from God?

At the deepest point in this person's brokenness and pain, how was he/she seen and loved by God?

How are we to relate to those who are broken or far from God?

Think of one person you need to love more fully.

What one thing can I do to love this person in a concrete way?

OUTSIDE THE GATES

God's Words

When he left there, he met Jehonadab son of Rechab coming to meet him; he greeted him, and said to him, "Is your heart as true to mine as mine is to yours?" Jehonadab answered, "It is." Jehu said, "If it is, give me your hand."

—2 Kings 10:15 (NRSV)

Wesley's Words

"The Need to be Right"

It is certain, so long as we know but *in part*, that all men will not see all things alike. It is an unavoidable consequence of the present weakness and shortness of human understanding, that several men will be of several minds in religion as well as in common life....Farther: Although every man necessarily believes that every particular opinion which he holds is true; (for to believe any opinion is not true, is the same thing as not to hold it;) yet can no man be assured that all his own opinions, taken together, are true. Nay, every thinking man is assured they are not; seeing . . "To be ignorant of many things, and to mistake in some, is the necessary condition of humanity." This, therefore, he is sensible, is his own case. He knows, in the general, that he himself is mistaken; although in what particulars he mistakes, he does not, perhaps he cannot, know.

I say, perhaps he cannot know; for who can tell how far invincible ignorance may extend? or (that comes to the same thing) invincible prejudice?—which is often so fixed in tender minds, that it is afterwards impossible to tear up what has taken so deep a root...

Every wise man, therefore, will allow others the same liberty of thinking which he desires they should allow him; and will no more insist on their embracing his opinions, than he would have them to insist on his embracing theirs. He bears with those who differ from him, and only asks him with whom he desires to unite in love that single question, "Is thy heart right, as my heart is with thy heart?"

—"Catholic Spirit," no. 39, 3–6

Contemporary Words

One of the main attitudes constraining churches from a healthy and growing focus on the mission field outside our gates is the ever-present need to "be right." We want to feel that what we believe is God's absolute and complete truth. Because of this belief, it is natural for us to see those who hold thoughts or beliefs that are different from ours as wrong. This attitude affects us on two fronts: first, it can allow us to miss our opportunity for mission if we remain clustered with others who think, act, and believe exactly as we do. Secondly, if this attitude of self-righteousness takes root inside the church, causing argument and divisiveness to characterize our community, it can cause us to miss the opportunity for effective witness as well.

DAY 2

—————————————— WEEK FOUR ——————————————

My Words

Think of a time when a disagreement in thought or belief has kept you from being open to reaching out to a person who was different from you.

Write a description of the situation.

Think of a time when you have seen a divisiveness within the church that prevents members from being a positive witness to those outside the church.

Record your thoughts and feelings about this situation.

Reread and underline the third paragraph in the "Wesley's Words" section on page 64.
What kind of difference would it make to my church if I were willing to "bear with those who differ," and offer my hand? Record your thoughts below.

OUTSIDE THE GATES

God's Words

What good is it, my brothers, if a man claims to have faith but has no deeds? Can such faith save him? Suppose a brother or sister is without clothes and daily food. If one of you says to him, "Go, I wish you well; keep warm and well fed," but does nothing about his physical needs, what good is it? In the same way, faith by itself, if it is not accompanied by action, is dead.

—James 2:14–17 (NIV)

Wesley's Words

"Can True Love be Passive?"

DAY 3

Is thy heart right toward thy neighbour? Dost thou love, as thyself, all mankind without exception? "If you love those only that love you, what thank have ye?" Do you "love your enemies?" Is your soul full of good-will, of tender affection, toward them? Do you love even the enemies of God, the unthankful and unholy? Do your bowels yearn over them? Could you "wish yourself" temporally "accursed" for their sake? And do you show this by "blessing them that curse you, and praying for those that despitefully use you and persecute you?"

Do you show your love by your works? While you have time, as you have opportunity, do you in fact "do good to all men," neighbours or strangers, friends or enemies, good or bad? Do you do them all the good you can; endeavouring to supply all their wants; assisting them both in body and soul, to the uttermost of your power?—If thou art thus minded, may every Christian say, yea, if thou art but sincerely desirous of it, and following on till thou attain, then "thy heart is right, as my heart is with thy heart."

—"Catholic Spirit," no. 39, 17–18

Contemporary Words

In James, we hear about the worthlessness of wishing hurting people well without trying to touch them at the point of their need. I believe that the same is true of love. If we simply say, we love as Jesus loved, but keep that love inside our churches or inside our minds, then we are missing the point. I once took a course in scuba diving. As part of the test for certification, we had to go to the bottom of the deepest part of the pool, remove our tanks, disassemble them, and breathe directly off the tank. I saw some people try to inhale the tiny stream of bubbles while under water and begin to cough. Those people shot to the surface with a purpose and passion I had not witnessed in them before. Their urge to preserve self became their central focus. In that light, let us ask, what does it mean to love your neighbor as yourself? I believe it has something to do with urgency and a willingness to act.

WEEK FOUR

My Words

Take a few moments to reflect upon the community surrounding your church.

Who lives "outside the gates" and who is different from you?

Ask Jesus to help you see them as he sees them. Spend time in prayer.

Ask Jesus to help you love them as he loves them. Spend time in prayer.

What actions can you think of that would appropriately express Christian love to these persons? List what you can do.

OUTSIDE THE GATES

God's Words

But God demonstrates his own love for us in this: While we were still sinners, Christ died for us.

—Romans 5:8 (NIV)

Wesley's Words

"Accepting each other as Christ has accepted us"

I do not mean, "Be of my opinion." You need not: I do not expect or desire it. Neither do I mean, "I will be of your opinion." I cannot: It does not depend on my choice: I can no more think, than I can see or hear, as I will. Keep you your opinion; I mine; and that as steadily as ever. You need not even endeavour to come over to me, or bring me over to you. I do not desire you to dispute those points, or to hear or speak one word concerning them. Let all opinions alone on one side and the other: Only "give me thine hand."

—"Catholic Spirit," no. 39, II.1

Contemporary Words

God's love for us is not based on our behavior or belief. God's love for us is unconditional. This kind of love is the model of love for people in God's community. The diversity of the early Methodist people was much like the diversity of the people who made up the early church. There were people of different religious traditions and differing schools of thought. There were people from various educational levels. There were people from every point on the socio-economic spectrum. In the midst of this complex mixture of people groups, it was very important for Wesley to help individuals develop an attitude of acceptance of people unlike themselves. It was this spirit of acceptance that provided the foundation for the new community in the midst of diversity.

────────── **WEEK FOUR**──────────

My Words

List some "opinions" that separate Christians.

Look again at the previous page. Read carefully and underline the sentence in the "Wesley's Words" section, beginning with "Keep you your opinion; I mine…"

Do you have a relationship with someone inside or outside the church in which you could practice this advice?

How would you begin?

OUTSIDE THE GATES

God's Words

Love is patient; love is kind; love is not envious or boastful or arrogant or rude. It does not insist on its own way; it is not irritable or resentful; it does not rejoice in wrongdoing, but rejoices in truth. It bears all things, believes all things, hopes all things, endures all things.

—1 Corinthians 13:4–7 (NRSV)

Wesley's Words

"Seeing With Eyes of Hope and Love"

Love me (but in a higher degree than thou dost the bulk of mankind) with the love that is *longsuffering and kind*; that is patient; if I am ignorant or out of the way, bearing and not increasing my burden; and is tender, soft, and compassionate still;—that *envieth not*, if at any time it please God to prosper me in his work even more than thee. Love me with the love that *is not provoked*, either at my follies or infirmities; or even at my acting (if it should sometimes so appear to thee) not according to the will of God. Love me so as to *think no evil* of me; to put away all jealousy and evil-surmising. Love me with the love that *covereth all things*; that never reveals either my faults or infirmities;—that *believeth all things*; is always willing to think the best, to put the fairest construction on all my words and actions;—that *hopeth all things*; either that the thing related was never done; or not done with such circumstances as are related; or, at least, that it was done with a good intention, or in a sudden stress of temptation. And hope to the end, that whatever is amiss, will, by the grace of God, be corrected; and whatever is wanting, supplied, through the riches of his mercy in Christ Jesus.

—"Catholic Spirit," no. 39, II. 4

DAY 5

Contemporary Words

It is so easy to look out from behind the walls of the church, or our homes, or our established communities and see those who are different as a threat to "life as we know it." Differences in thought, opinion, behavior, or belief often make us uncomfortable and quick to judge or distance ourselves from "them." Yet, it is to those who were different that Jesus went. It was with "them" that he spent his time. It was to them that he offered unconditional love, and it was for them that he eventually gave his life. In the same way, Wesley felt called and responded to those who were different, broken, and outside the context of the life of the church in that day. He tried to see people as Christ saw them, through the eyes of love and hope.

—————— WEEK FOUR ——————

My Words

Have you ever been in a situation wherein you were called on to love someone you were not naturally drawn to love? Describe the situation.

What did you find difficult?

What were the emotions you can remember?

How did you do?

What do you think it means that "Love bears all things, believes all things, hopes all things and endures all things?"

---------- **NOTES** ----------

Endnotes

[1] Carole King and James Taylor, *Mudslide Slim and Blue Horizon*, Warner Brothers Records, W22561, 1971.

5 CLEAR EXPECTATIONS

We Each Play a Part

For we are God's servants, working together; you are God's field, God's building.

—*1 Corinthians 3:9 (NRSV)*

CLEAR EXPECTATIONS

We Each Play a Part

The news is not good. His cholesterol numbers are off the chart. His blood pressure indicators are soaring way beyond the safe level. "The doctor told me I am a walking time-bomb" are the words that come from the mouth of my twenty-six-year-old best friend. "Is there anything I can do to help?" I ask. "Well, yes, as a matter of fact there is. You can get up every morning and ride bikes with me for an hour before class." (This is one of those moments like at dinner when you see the last piece of chicken on the plate—you know you want it, but, because it is the right thing to do, you ask, "Anyone want this last piece?" and someone says "yes"...) I mean, after all, it is Denver, Colorado, in the winter. It is frigid. There is snow. Class starts at 8:00 A.M., which means getting out of the warmth of the bed before the sun is up, bundling up in layers, unimagined when I lived in Atlanta. It means facing wind chill that would double its chilly bite as we plunged through the icy air, wheeling our way toward Washington Park to see geese sitting on the frozen lake. It is one of those moments wherein it seems easier and more enjoyable to pretend that we have no connection with those close to us, or that we have no responsibility to help those with whom we have been given the journey of life. It would seem easier to stay in bed, but there on the bike, daily, as the sun breaks over the Denver skyline and splashes upon the face of the Rocky Mountains, two bundled seminary students, dressed like sleeping bags, learn the power of accountability.

Most of us have good intentions. Most of us are also extremely capable of being distracted from fulfilling those intentions. There were many mornings there in Denver, I am sure, that if I had not had my friend waiting for me out at the bike rack, I would have been able to rationalize some good reason to stay in bed just a little longer. There were many mornings, I am sure, that if my friend had not known that I would be knocking on his door, waking his wife and him if he left me standing alone at the bike rack, that he would have been able to conjure in his mind some good reason to stay in bed just a little longer. Yet, as with mountain climbers who, while roped to another climber, ascend to heights they would not attempt alone, we daily met and rode, lost weight and got healthy, and in the process watched, up close, the winter turning to spring. We saw the beauty of dew covered tulips at sunrise pushing their heads through melting snow as those same geese balanced upon the last pieces of ice which had solidly covered the lake a month before. We raced each other. We discussed classes. We discussed theology and faith. Instead of an extra hour under the blanket, we shared experiences of the unfolding beauty of the creative hand of God and in the midst of it, shared questions, thoughts, fears, doubts, hopes, and dreams. Not a bad trade.

Excitement, dreams, decisions, and intention all have value, yet without accountability, they are apt never to get past our ability to convince ourselves that it would be easier to stay in bed just a little longer. Accountability is a powerful force. It was a powerful force in the development of the Methodist movement.

George Whitfield, a contemporary of John Wesley, was one of the most dynamic and powerful preachers of the day. He was known for his ability to draw a crowd and leave them "spell-bound." His preaching in Bristol stirred the fire that became a large-scale revival. Whitfield preached for conversion and was very effective. Thousands of people responded to the call to "turn to Christ." He drew the crowds, held their attention, captured their imaginations and called for conversion. The crowds responded. Thousands of people were called to new life. Thousands of people responded. Thousands experienced conversion.

If the purpose is simply to get people to make a decision for Christ then "revival preaching" would be enough. If, however, the purpose is to bring people into a relationship with Christ that transforms their lives and the world around them in a lasting way, then something is needed to sustain the activity and commitment that otherwise would fade as soon as the immediate experience of the conversion has faded. Something more than "revival" preaching is needed. Something more than individual conversion is required. This is where John Wesley's understanding of accountability, discipleship formation, and leadership development, coupled with organizational genius, emerged as an answer to the need.

In the context of this new ministry, Wesley remembered words spoken to him when he was younger that had shaped his understanding of the journey of discipleship. "Sir, you wish to serve God and go to heaven. Remember that you cannot serve Him alone. You must therefore find companions or make them. The Bible knows nothing of solitary religion."[1] This understanding was what motivated his leadership of the Holy Club at Oxford. He knew that the fire of conversion was soon extinguished if it was left to burn alone, but when combined with others who were like-minded, the chances for success were much greater.

This week, our readings will focus on the development of the process of discipleship formation and leadership development that Wesley developed around the idea of accountability in the midst of ministry.

CLEAR EXPECTATIONS

God's Words

But you are a chosen people, a royal priesthood, a holy nation, a people belonging to God, that you may declare the praises of him who called you out of darkness into his wonderful light. Once you were not a people, but now you are the people of God; once you had not received mercy, but now you have received mercy.

—1 Peter 2:9–10 (NIV)

Wesley's Words

"Royal Priesthood, Holy Nation"

He is raising up those of every age and degree, young men and maidens, old men and children, to be "a chosen generation, a royal priesthood, a holy nation, a peculiar people; to show forth His praise, who hath called them out of darkness into his marvelous light." And we have no reason to doubt, but he will continue so to do, till the great promise is fulfilled; till "the earth is filled with the knowledge of the glory of the Lord, as the waters cover the sea; till all Israel is saved, and the fullness of the Gentiles is come in."

"Wisdom of God's Counsels," no. 68, 23

DAY 1

Contemporary Words

Although Wesley had grown up in a minister's family and was very familiar with the rules of the church, he developed a profound sense of the importance of the ministry of the laity. At first, he was hesitant about allowing those who were not ordained by the church to be ones who proclaimed the Gospel, but his mother encouraged him not to react to the idea without first looking to see if the preaching bore fruit. As Wesley witnessed the growth of the movement and the increasing demands and opportunities for preaching and ministry, he spent more time and effort developing leaders from among the converts. Wesley's itinerant preachers were often laymen and sometimes even laywomen. The Wesleyan revival was a powerful example of the ministry in the hands of the laity with the clergy providing leadership, organization and the sacraments. The work of the church was in the hands of the people and the people were the priests.

This idea of the priesthood of all believers provides us with an important dimension of identity that so often is missing in church. As part of God's royal priesthood, we are gifted to serve and given opportunities for service as well as responsibility to serve as bearers of God's activity in the world.

WEEK FIVE

My Words

What does it mean for you to be a member of a congregation? What does it mean for you to be a follower of Christ? How does it inform your identity? Does it give you a particular purpose or direction?

Read the following paragraph from The United Methodist Book of Discipline[2] *and answer the following questions in light of this paragraph.*

¶ 219. All members of Christ's universal church are called to share in the ministry which is committed to the whole church of Jesus Christ. Therefore, each member of The United Methodist Church is to be a servant of Christ on mission in the local and worldwide community. This servanthood is performed in family life, daily work, recreation and social activities, responsible citizenship, the stewardship of property and accumulated resources, the issues of corporate life, and all attitudes toward other persons. Participation in disciplined groups is an expected part of personal mission involvement. Each member is called upon to be a witness for Christ in the world, a light and leaven in society, and a reconciler in a culture of conflict. Each member is to identify with the agony and suffering of the world and to radiate and exemplify the Christ of hope. The standards of attitude and conduct set forth in the Social Principles (Part IV) shall be considered as an essential resource for guiding each member of the Church in being a servant of Christ on mission.

What is the role of a layperson?

What does it mean for me to be a member of a royal priesthood?

CLEAR EXPECTATIONS

God's Words

Enlarge the site of your tent, and let the curtains of your habitations be stretched out; do not hold back; lengthen your cords and strengthen your stakes. For you will spread out to the right and to the left, and your descendants will possess the nations and will settle the desolate towns.

—Isaiah 54:2–3 (NRSV)

Wesley's Words

"Building to House the Ministry"

We took possession of a piece of ground, near St. James's church-yard, in the Horse Fair, where it was designed to build a room, large enough to contain both the societies of Nicholas and Baldwin-Street, and such of their acquaintance as might desire to be present with them, at such times as the Scripture was expounded. And on Saturday, 12, the first stone was laid, with the voice of praise and thanksgiving.

—*Journal*, May 9, 1739

DAY 2

Contemporary Words

Even though, as a "Fellow" of Lincoln College at Oxford, Wesley supposedly had the approval and the authority of the church to preach in any pulpit in the land, he found himself barred from churches all across the country. People saw him as a radical who took the religion thing too seriously. There were even several instances of mobs attacking him while he was preaching or stoning houses where his meetings were held. In the face of this controversy Wesley didn't lose hope or focus but forged ahead and took steps to ensure that the ministry that was happening would not be derailed. He didn't build a church building in the traditional sense of the term, but he did build a building that was well designed to house the work of a movement.

The New Room in Bristol was at once a meeting house for the new converts, a mission center for ministry with the poor, and a training house and residence for the much-needed new generation of leadership. It may look rather simple to us today, but it was creatively designed, efficient, and as "high-tech" as any structure of its era. It was designed to house a different model of training than the type Wesley experienced at Oxford, but it was a model of education and training that kept those who were responding to the call close to the ministry field, in service, and meeting needs as they learned to lead. The New Room was a building designed to accomplish the purpose of the church, instead of a building that, as so often is the case, shapes the ministry of the people who gather there.

WEEK FIVE

My Words

Reflect upon these questions and write your responses below each section.

What characteristics do you look for in leaders?

What kind of characteristics do you look for in a layperson in church leadership? How do you identify and develop leaders in your church?

What is needed for someone to be a good pastor?

When was the last time someone entered into pastoral ministry from your church?

CLEAR EXPECTATIONS

God's Words

Bear with one another and, if anyone has a complaint against another, forgive each other; just as the Lord has forgiven you, so you also must forgive. Above all, clothe yourselves with love, which binds everything together in perfect harmony. And let the peace of Christ rule in your hearts, to which indeed you were called in the one body. And be thankful. Let the word of Christ dwell in you richly; teach and admonish one another in all wisdom; and with gratitude in your hearts sing psalms, hymns, and spiritual songs to God. And whatever you do, in word or deed, do everything in the name of the Lord Jesus, giving thanks to God the Father through him.

—Colossians 3:13–17 (NRSV)

Wesley's Words

"Gathering for Accountable Discipleship"

Such a society is no other than "a company of men having the form and seeking the power of godliness, united in order to pray together, to receive the word of exhortation, and to watch over one another in love, that they may help each other to work out their salvation."

That it may the more easily be discerned, whether they are indeed working out their own salvation, each society is divided into smaller companies, called classes, according to their respective places of abode. There are about twelve persons in every class; one of whom is styled *the Leader*. It is his business, (1.) To see each person in his class once a week at least, in order to inquire how their souls prosper; to advise, reprove, comfort, or exhort, as occasion may require; to receive what they are willing to give toward the relief of the poor. (2.) To meet the Minister and the Stewards of the society once a week; in order to inform the Minister of any that are sick, or of any that walk disorderly, and will not be reproved; to pay to the Stewards what they have received of their several classes in the week preceding; and to show their account of what each person has contributed.

—"The Nature, Design, and General Rules of the United Societies," 2–3

Contemporary Words

The class meeting was designed for the care and accountability of the people. It was where people had their close, face-to-face relationships and were able to ask questions and have discussions that enabled their faith to grow. It was the group that provided Christian care for one another during illness or the loss of a job. The class leader was one of their own who had been given training in the care of the group. Together, they could strive to live out new life in Christ. Together they had a better chance at succeeding than they did alone.

DAY 3

WEEK FIVE

My Words

The class meetings provided people with an opportunity to discuss the struggles that all people face, yet most hide. It was this ability to discuss that gave them the strength and encouragement to attempt to live more faithfully. The questions used during the meetings seem very direct, but they were effective. Spend some time with the questions below and respond in writing to each of them. If there is something that comes to mind that you don't want to write about, ask yourself "why?" and consider what it would be like if you had a person or group with whom you could openly discuss your struggles.

1. What known sins have you committed since our last meeting?

2. What temptations have you met with?

3. How were you delivered?

4. What have you thought, said, or done, of which you doubt whether it be sin or not?

CLEAR EXPECTATIONS

God's Words

Do not be deceived; God is not mocked, for you reap whatever you sow. If you sow to your own flesh, you will reap corruption from the flesh; but if you sow to the Spirit, you will reap eternal life from the Spirit. So let us not grow weary in doing what is right, for we will reap at harvest time, if we do not give up. So then, whenever we have an opportunity, let us work for the good of all, and especially for those of the family of faith.

—Galatians 6:7–10 (NRSV)

Wesley's Words

"Salt and Light"

There is one only condition previously required in those who desire admission into these societies,—a desire "to flee from the wrath to come, to be saved from their sins:" But, wherever this is really fixed in the soul, it will be shown by its fruits. It is therefore expected of all who continue therein, that they should continue to evidence their desire of salvation. First, by doing no harm, by avoiding evil in every kind; especially that which is most generally practiced ....Secondly, by doing good, by being, in every kind, merciful after their power; as they have opportunity, doing good of every possible sort, and as far as is possible, to all men...

—"The Nature, Design, and General Rules of the United Societies," 4–5

DAY 4

Contemporary Words

It is very important to provide clear expectations for those who are choosing to be followers of Christ. The leaders of the class meetings are serious about keeping people accountable to growth in the Christian life. Providing clear expectations is not an overly zealous way to impose a particular moral standard; it is a set of boundaries in which one could not only live in healthy community and spiritual growth but also make a difference in the lives of others. Followers are to be those who not only avoid evil but also do all the good they could find to do. What a difference in perspective and possibility emerges from persons who are struggling for survival in a "look-out-for-number-one world," and through Christ, find themselves striving for holiness with a group of supportive people!

— WEEK FIVE —

My Words

Consider that you are hearing the following instructions as part of the expectations of membership in your church. **What, specifically, would they mean to your life? What do you find meaningful? What do you find problematic? Write your responses below each section.**

DIRECTIONS GIVEN TO THE BAND-SOCIETIES DECEMBER 25, 1744

You are supposed to have the faith that "overcometh the world."
To you, therefore, it is not grievous,—

I. Carefully to abstain from doing evil; in particular,—

1. Neither to buy nor sell anything at all on the Lord's day.

2. To taste no spirituous liquor, no dram of any kind, unless prescribed by a Physician.

3. To be at a word both in buying and selling.

4. To pawn nothing, no, not to save life.

5. Not to mention the fault of any behind his back, and to stop those short that do.

6. To wear no needless ornaments, such as rings, earrings, necklaces, lace, ruffles.

7. To use no needless self-indulgence, such as taking snuff or tobacco, unless prescribed by a Physician.

II. Zealously to maintain good works; in particular,—

1. To give alms of such things as you possess, and that to the uttermost of your power.

2. To reprove all that sin in your sight, and that in love and meekness of wisdom.

3. To be patterns of diligence and frugality, of self-denial, and taking up the cross daily.

CLEAR EXPECTATIONS

God's Words

Let us hold fast to the confession of our hope without wavering, for he who has promised is faithful. And let us consider how to provoke one another to love and good deeds, not neglecting to meet together, as is the habit of some, but encouraging one another, and all the more as you see the Day approaching.

—Hebrews 10:23–25 (NRSV)

Wesley's Words

"Clear Expectations"

It is expected of all who desire to continue in these societies, that they should continue to evidence their desire of salvation, Thirdly, by attending upon all the ordinances of God. Such are, the public worship of God; the ministry of the word, either read or expounded; the supper of the Lord; family and private prayer; searching the Scriptures; and fasting, or abstinence.

These are the General Rules of our societies; all which we are taught of God to observe, even in his written word, the only rule, and the sufficient rule, both of our faith and practice. And all these, we know, his Spirit writes on every truly awakened heart. If there be any among us who observe them not, who habitually break any of them, let it be made known unto them who watch over that soul as they that must give an account. We will admonish him of the error of his ways; we will bear with him for a season: But then if he repent not, he hath no more place among us. We have delivered our own souls.

—"The Nature, Design, Rules of the United Societies," 6–7

DAY 5

Contemporary Words

Membership was meaningful in the societies because it made a difference and it had clear expectations. People were motivated to work through the process of individual transformation and to enter into a ministry activity that would make a difference in the world around them because these expectations were clearly defined and there was accountability. Low expectations produce low commitment and yield poor results. High expectations produce high commitment and yield good results. What does this idea of clear expectations say to us as a church today?

Week Five

My Words

If someone were to ask you the following questions about your church how would you respond? Write your answers in the space provided below.

What must I do to become a member?

What are the expectations of me as a member?

What happens if I don't fulfill the expectations?

NOTES

Endnotes

1 Percy Livingstone Parker, ed. *The Journal of John Wesley* (Chicago: Moody Press, 1951), p.20.

2 *The United Methodist Book of Discipline 2000* (Nashville: The United Methodist Publishing House, 2000), pp.131–132.

6 THE EMERGING CHURCH

Uncovering Our Ancient Future

"My people have committed two sins:
They have forsaken me,
the spring of living water,
and have dug their own cisterns,
broken cisterns that cannot hold water."

—*Jeremiah 2:13 (NIV)*

THE EMERGING CHURCH

Uncovering Our Ancient Future

The sunlight filtered into the room in soft warm stripes sliced by the Venetian blinds hanging in the window and fell across the faces of the people, some kneeling, some standing with hands open, some praying, some singing. It was a moment of prayer and consecration. It was a moment of recognition. Surrounded by towering pines and the foothills of the ancient Appalachian Mountains in a valley named "resting place," or *Sumatanga* in the language of the Native Americans who originally inhabited the area, we had come to learn and grow as faithful church leaders, as ministers both clergy and lay, in this time of great change and challenge. We had gathered for a closing service of communion and consecration.

The Bishop had come to bless and commission those who were completing their training at the Academy for Congregational Development. His sermon was designed to challenge the participants, to commission them for their work, and to send them out with a calling to be the church today, whatever that may look like...to focus on making disciples and not on maintaining institutions. He told of the powerful effect the church had had on his life and on the world around him as he was growing up. He told the difficult truth about the state in which many churches find themselves today—people getting older and fewer in numbers, people wondering why there were no young people coming and worried about the future of the church. He spoke directly to these leaders and, with passion, called them to lead in ways that would reach out beyond the walls of the church and do the work of God in their neighborhoods, cities, and towns. I liked his talk. It resonated with me at a deep level.

After the sermon, the participants came forward for a time of blessing and commissioning and during that time, they participated in a renewal of their baptismal vows. They felt again the touch of the water, and remembered that with that water, the symbol of Baptism, came not only a new life characterized by grace and forgiveness, but also a new life characterized by the entrance into the priesthood of all believers. In the touch of that water, they were reminded that they were part of the Body of Christ, and given gifts for service and the building up of the body. The Bishop had brought a bowl to hold the water for the baptismal renewal. It was a special bowl that had been given to him as a gift when he was in Africa. He had used it for this purpose on many occasions. Beautiful, hand-carved wood sat on the table, between the candles holding the water that told the story of redemption and new life.

As my wife played the piano and led the music for this closing service and the participants filed forward, I watched prayerfully. It was beautiful to see. They were taking it seriously. They were soaking it in. They were alive and ready to be touched and sent out for God. After talking about the challenge, after praying over the water as a symbol of God's Holy Spirit and the power to renew, he called people forward to renew their covenant.

Then it happened. Something that could not be planned happened that spoke to me louder than words. I was sitting on the side. As a leader for the weekend retreat, I was helping with the music and was waiting for the other participants to go forward. I noticed a drip of water coming off of the table. I watched the drips increase. Something had spilled. I looked more closely. I don't know how, but during the prayer for the water and for the renewal and reformation of the church, that beautiful old wooden bowl that had held so much memory and had held so much meaning had split and the water was pouring out on the floor. At first I thought, "how terrible...," but then I saw the gift.

What a powerful symbol!

> ...that beautiful old wooden bowl that had held so much memory and had held so much meaning had split and the water was pouring out on the floor.

Sometimes the structures we have designed as instruments to share the life-giving message of God split, no matter how beautiful they are, no matter how useful and meaningful they have been, no matter how much we love them. Sometimes they split. They cease to function as they once had, like the church in Wesley's day. At that point we have choices. One choice is to be so attached to the bowl for nostalgic or sentimental or loyalty reasons that we hang on to the bowl as the water drains away. Another choice is to try to repair, or get a new bowl so we can do what is really important—the faithful sharing of that powerful truth that has come to us alive from the past which is our responsibility to deliver, with all of its life, to children and grandchildren yet to come. "I will pour out my Spirit," says the Lord. What is the state of our bowl?

During this final week, we will be looking at readings from the scripture and readings from Wesley's writings that emerge out of times of rebuilding when the bowls had cracked. Through the scriptures we will look at the return of those who had been exiled from the Promised Land and their rebuilding of the Temple. We will also look at the concluding challenge in Wesley's sermon that was delivered to the people who gathered on the day they laid the foundation for the City Road Chapel in London. It is a challenge that was given to those who had either witnessed or had participated in one of the greatest renewal movements ever experienced in the history of Christianity. In both of these situations, the people were called to faithfulness. They were called to difficult faithfulness and commitment in an important time of change.

THE EMERGING CHURCH

God's Words

This is what the LORD says: "Stand at the crossroads and look; ask for the ancient paths, ask where the good way is, and walk in it, and you will find rest for your souls.

—Jeremiah 6:16 (NIV)

Contemporary Words

In the words of the prophet Jeremiah, spoken to the people of Israel just before the exile, there was heard a call to return to the "ancient paths." The same message was spoken by John Wesley. Wesley was a defender of what was called "Primitive Christianity." He believed that the truth of Christianity, as well as the model for faithfulness in the future, was to be found in the past—in the model of church found in the book of Acts. The renewal in the days of Wesley was brought about by a return to the "ancient paths." Today, there are many churches that, once again, are returning to this model and looking to the past for a roadmap to the future. I believe the emerging effective church in the twenty-first century will be a church with an ancient future.

DAY 1

Wesley's Words

How is Your Experience?

All of the "Wesley's Words" sections in this chapter are taken from the concluding challenge in the sermon written on the day the foundation was laid for the new chapel headquarters in London. The readings do not correspond directly with the Scripture and the commentary; however, I have placed the words here as a fitting challenge for us as we consider how we will live in this time of change and choice.

Brethren, I presume the greater part of you also are members of the Church of England. So, at least, you are called; but you are not so indeed, unless you are witnesses of the religion above described. And are you really such? Judge not one another; but every man look into his own bosom. How stands the matter in your own breast? Examine your conscience before God. Are you a happy partaker of this scriptural, this truly primitive, religion? Are you a witness of the religion of love? Are you a lover of God and all mankind?

—"On Laying the Foundation of the New Chapel," no. 132, 17

WEEK SIX

My Words

John considered himself to be a defender of primitive Christianity as recorded in the book of Acts. Read the passage below and underline the practices of the early church that illustrate for you the heart of Christianity.

They devoted themselves to the apostles' teaching and to the fellowship, to the breaking of bread and to prayer. Everyone was filled with awe, and many wonders and miraculous signs were done by the apostles. All the believers were together and had everything in common. Selling their possessions and goods, they gave to anyone as he had need. Every day they continued to meet together in the temple courts. They broke bread in their homes and ate together with glad and sincere hearts, praising God and enjoying the favor of all the people. And the Lord added to their number daily those who were being saved.

—Acts 2:42–47 (NIV)

Journal your responses to the following questions:

Which elements in the above passage are present in your religious life?

Which elements are missing?

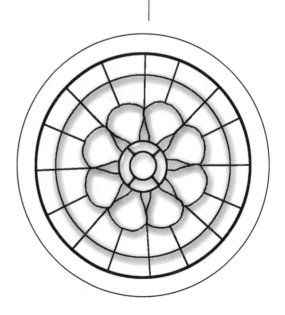

THE EMERGING CHURCH

God's Words

This is what Cyrus king of Persia says:

"The LORD, the God of heaven, has given me all the kingdoms of the earth and he has appointed me to build a temple for him at Jerusalem in Judah. Anyone of his people among you—may his God be with him, and let him go up to Jerusalem in Judah and build the temple of the LORD, the God of Israel, the God who is in Jerusalem. And the people of any place where survivors may now be living are to provide him with silver and gold, with goods and livestock, and with freewill offerings for the temple of God in Jerusalem."

—Ezra 1:2–4 (NIV)

Contemporary Words

In despair, in exile, suddenly there is a ray of hope. "We can go home?!"

Some of the Israelites knew where home was and what it was like. They had been alive when they were forced to leave. They are elated to be going home, but know deep down that it will be difficult because it would not be the same as when they had left it.

Others had only heard stories about "home." They had grown up knowing nothing but life in exile. Their place of exile was home, and they were not sure that going back to their ancestral "home" would be worth the effort.

It was to these people that the call to return home came. The people of God were called to pick up what they had been doing for seventy years, to make the long journey back to the ancient place, and to begin the work of rebuilding what had once stood to the glory of God.

DAY 2

Wesley's Words

"How is Your Witness?"

Does your heart glow with gratitude to the Giver of every good and perfect gift, the Father of the spirits of all flesh, who giveth you life, and breath, and all things; who hath given you his Son, his only Son, that you "might not perish, but have everlasting life?" Is your soul warm with benevolence to all mankind? Do you long to have all men virtuous and happy? And does the constant tenor of your life and conversation bear witness of this?

—"On Laying the Foundation of the New Chapel," no. 132, 17

WEEK SIX

My Words

The world the Israelites encountered in exile was a very different world from the Promised Land. The experience of the people who remembered the Promised Land was very different from the experience of those who had only known exile. I believe there are some similarities between those groups and the different generations that populate our churches today.

In *Resident Aliens*,[1] Will Willimon and Stanley Hauerwas point to a time, very different from today, when I believe the church felt at home and in its "Promised Land:"

> You see, our parents had never worried about whether we would grow up Christian. The church was the only show in town. On Sundays, the town closed down. One could not even buy a gallon of gas. There was a traffic jam on Sunday mornings at 9:45, when all went to their respective Sunday schools. By overlooking much that was wrong in the world—it was a racially segregated world, remember—people saw a world that looked good and right...Church, home, and state formed a national consortium that worked together to instill "Christian values." People grew up Christian simply by being born in places like Greenville, South Carolina, or Pleasant Grove, Texas.
>
> —*Resident Aliens*, p. 16

When you were growing up, was the church in the Promised Land, or was it in exile? Explain your answer.

Write about your memories of what it was like to be a child going to church.

What is different today for children and youth as they come to church?

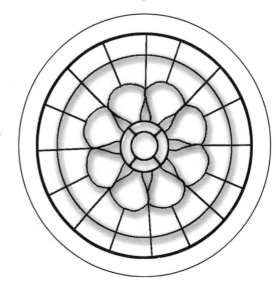

THE EMERGING CHURCH

God's Words

When the seventh month came and the Israelites had settled in their towns, the people assembled as one man in Jerusalem. Then Jeshua son of Jozadak and his fellow priests and Zerubbabel son of Shealtiel and his associates began to build the altar of the God of Israel to sacrifice burnt offerings on it, in accordance with what is written in the Law of Moses the man of God. Despite their fear of the peoples around them, they built the altar on its foundation and sacrificed burnt offerings on it to the LORD, both the morning and evening sacrifices. Then in accordance with what is written, they celebrated the Feast of Tabernacles with the required number of burnt offerings prescribed for each day. After that, they presented the regular burnt offerings, the New Moon sacrifices and the sacrifices for all the appointed sacred feasts of the LORD, as well as those brought as freewill offerings to the LORD. On the first day of the seventh month they began to offer burnt offerings to the LORD, though the foundation of the LORD'S temple had not yet been laid.

—Ezra 3:1–6 (NIV)

DAY 3

Contemporary Words

Those who responded to the call to rebuild God's temple knew how important their task was. They knew that it would take more than their own efforts. They knew that the venture would be successful only if it was powerfully connected to God and emerged from a responsiveness to the direction and will of God. Before they started rebuilding, before they laid the foundation, they built an altar and made their offerings to God. Wesley also knew that religion was nothing if it was only words, beliefs, and lifeless ritual. He believed that what was needed was a faith which was rooted in a living relationship with God and which was lived out in every dimension of daily life.

Wesley's Words

"How is Your Love?"

Do you "love, not in word" only, "but in deed and in truth?" Do you persevere in the "work of faith, and the labour of love?" Do you "walk in love, as Christ also loved us, and gave himself for us?" Do you, as you have time, "do good unto all men;" and in as high a degree as you are able? *Whosoever thus* "doeth the will of my Father which is in heaven, the same is my brother, and sister, and mother."

—"On Laying the Foundation of the New Chapel," no. 132, 17

WEEK SIX

My Words

Before launching into the project of rebuilding, the people of God spent time in prayer and in the offering of sacrifices. Ask God to show you how your church might be better equipped or aligned to reach out to younger generations.

Spend ten minutes in silence listening, then write your thoughts in the space below.

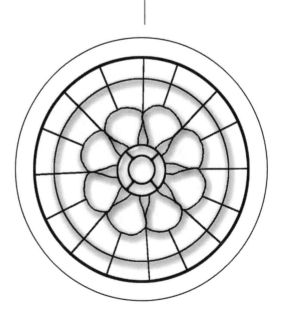

THE EMERGING CHURCH

God's Words

When the builders laid the foundation of the temple of the LORD, the priests in their vestments and with trumpets, and the Levites (the sons of Asaph) with cymbals, took their places to praise the LORD, as prescribed by David king of Israel. With praise and thanksgiving they sang to the LORD:
"He is good;
his love to Israel endures forever."

—Ezra 3:10–11 (NIV)

Contemporary Words

What a day that must have been. Everyone was gathered together to witness something that had started with a call from God and a response of a faithful people. It took faith. It took prayer. It took commitment. But most of all, it took being willing to step out and move in the direction to which God was calling, and go where God already was. Armed with that kind of faith and the knowledge that "God's love endures forever," they were able to reconnect with God for the renewal of God's people.

Wesley's Words

"How is Your Longing?"

Whosoever thou art, whose heart is herein as my heart, give me thine hand! Come, and let us magnify the Lord together, and labour to promote his kingdom upon earth! Let us join hearts and hands in this blessed work, in striving to bring glory to God in the highest, by establishing peace and good will among men, to the uttermost of our power! First. Let our hearts be joined herein; let us unite our wishes and prayers; let our whole soul pant after a general revival of pure religion and undefiled, the restoration of the image of God, pure love, in every child of man!

—"On Laying the Foundation of the New Chapel," no. 132, 17

———— WEEK SIX ————

My Words

Think of someone from a previous generation who greatly affected your life or faith.

Write that person's name and something about him or her that affected you.

Think about someone in a younger generation who is important to you. Think about what can you do for that person, or for others in that age group, that would positively affect their lives and help them develop a strong sense of the goodness and enduring love of God.

Write down the name of the person and list some things you might be able to do to positively affect this person's life. (*List as many individuals as you like.*)

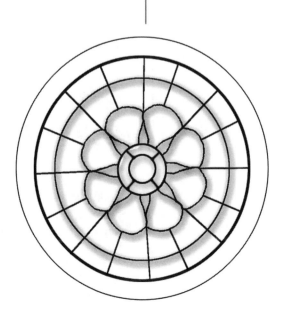

THE EMERGING CHURCH

God's Words

And all the people gave a great shout of praise to the LORD, because the foundation of the house of the LORD was laid. But many of the older priests and Levites and family heads, who had seen the former temple, wept aloud when they saw the foundation of this temple being laid, while many others shouted for joy. No one could distinguish the sound of the shouts of joy from the sound of weeping, because the people made so much noise. And the sound was heard far away.

—Ezra 3:11–13 (NIV)

Contemporary Words

Imagine that sound. Imagine the sound of thousands of people—trumpets sounding, cymbals crashing—and a sound rising from the crowd that was somewhat confusing.

Some of the people who were old enough to remember the Temple, upon seeing the foundation of the new one built on the rubble of the old, were overcome with sorrow. They broke down and filled the air with weeping and wailing. They knew that a new temple had to be built in order to transfer faith from generation to generation, but it was difficult to see the old one pass away.

The others, who had been born in captivity, who had never seen the old temple, and who, for the first time, were seeing the work of God unfold in the world through their efforts and sacrifices, were overflowing with joy. Their shouts filled the air with cheers and with laughter. Imagine that sound.

Cymbals and trumpets, weeping and cheering—so loud that you could hear them far away. What a day that must have been. It was a day of struggle and fulfillment, a day of pain and joy. Different generations worked, prayed, and sacrificed together; and from different memories and perspectives combined their efforts to insure that the love of God would be passed on to generations yet to come.

Wesley's Words

"How is Your Action?"

Then let us endeavour to promote, in our several stations, this scriptural, primitive religion; let us, with all diligence, diffuse the religion of love among all we have any intercourse with; let us provoke all men, not to enmity and contention, but to love and to good works; always remembering those deep words, (God engrave them on all our hearts!) "God is love; and he that dwelleth in love dwelleth in God, and God in him!"

—"On Laying the Foundation of the New Chapel," no. 132, 17

—————————— **WEEK SIX** ——————————

My Words

Close your eyes and imagine that day recorded in the book of Ezra on which the foundation had been laid and there was great celebration and sadness. What made people happy? What made them sad?

With this in mind, read the following questions and journal your responses.

As you look at some of the challenges facing our church in the present day:

1) What are some things that make you feel like the ones who had been part of the old Temple and hated to see it pass away?

2) What are some things that cause you to be happy and excited as you look at the new things that God is calling churches to do in order to reach out to new generations?

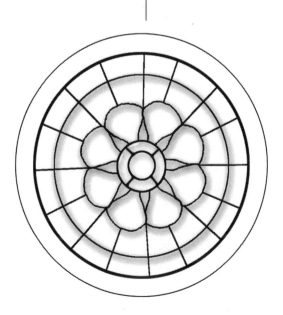

NOTES

Endnotes

[1] William H. Willimon and Stanley Hauerwas, *Resident Aliens: Life in the Christian Colony* (Nashville: Abingdon Press, 1990).

7 LET'S ROLL

Living Out the Vision In the Local Church

"Let's roll."

—*Todd Beamer, 9/11/01 before leading the passengers to wrestle control from the terrorist hijackers.*

"A journey of ten thousand miles begins with a single step."

—*Anonymous proverb*

Session 7

LET'S ROLL

Living Out the Vision In Our Congregation

The final section is to be completed during the closing session after watching the video. These pages contain an invitation to pray for your church and its ministry as well as an invitation to open your heart and mind to dream God's dreams for you. After spending time in prayer and reflection, you will have an opportunity to share ideas with the group.

The next steps in the process are up to you. This journey can have been a fun learning experience, or it can be the beginning of renewal for you, your congregation, and maybe even the church as a whole. In the following pages, you will find some suggestions on how to use what you have learned to help others share the vision for a dynamic renewal of the church as in the days of John Wesley. Please take some time to read the following section, to pray, and to share your ideas with one another.

Pray

Either as a group or individually, commit to pray for your church and its ministry. Pray and listen to God for direction and energy.

Write words or phrases that come to mind as you ask God about the future of your church. (*Remember that God, through prevenient grace, is already there; our job is to go where God already is.*)

How is God speaking to me at this time about my life of faith and the life of my church?

Who are those outside the gates of our church with whom we may be being called into ministry?

If there is nothing standing in the way, what would God be calling me and/or our congregation to do?

Where do I see the ministry of my congregation in five, ten, fifteen, or twenty years?

What are my "God-sized dreams" for the life and ministry of our congregation?

My Next Steps

Write down three things that you can agree to do right away to help your congregation move into God's future.